THE IMPORTANCE OF ONE

THE IMPORTANCE OF ONE

by

FLORENCE ZELDIN

KTAV PUBLISHING HOUSE, INC.

ISBN 87068-317-9

© COPYRIGHT 1980
KTAV PUBLISHING HOUSE, INC.

MANUFACTURED IN THE UNITED STATES OF AMERICA

CONTENTS

8 **JACOB BARSIMSON**
  The Right to Serve
15 **URIAH LEVY**
  Fighting the United States Navy
22 **ERNESTINE ROSE**
  The Lady with the Petitions
30 **JOSEPH GOLDBERGER**
  An Immigrant Makes His Mark
36 **NATHAN STRAUS**
  The Great Giver
44 **LILLIAN WALD**
  The Superwoman of Henry Street
52 **LOUIS BRANDEIS**
  Advocate of the People
60 **MORDECAI ANILEWITZ**
  Uprising
69 **HENRIETTA SZOLD**
  Helpful Henrietta
77 **LOUISE WATERMAN WISE**
  The Story of Louise
84 **CHAIM WEIZMANN**
  The Chemist
93 **EDDIE CANTOR**
  For Everybody's Benefit
100 **MOE BERG**
  The Smart Baseball Player
108 **RABBI LEO BAECK**
  The Keeper of His People
116 **DAVID SARNOFF**
  The Great Communicator
122 **GOLDA MEIR**
  The Lady Who Was Prime Minister
133 **ANSWERS**

To my granddaughters, Sivan and Sasha. May they grow up knowing the importance of one but respecting the rights of all.

INTRODUCTION

How many times have you heard someone say: "What can I do? I'm only one person." How often have you said it yourself? You find someone is being treated unfairly. You hear of people being sick. You learn about unhappy people. You think it would be great if something could be done to make life easier and happier for them. There are so many problems in the world around you, but you are only one person. What can you do to change things? True, you can't change everything—but you can try to change at least one. As the Talmud says: You don't have to do it all, but neither are you excused from beginning to do something.

The following chapters will tell you about some Jewish men and women who didn't like the things they saw happening. People's civil rights were being withheld. Employers were taking advantage of workers. The poor were living in bad, unhealthy conditions. People were suffering. Each of the men and women you will read about decided that these wrongs should be corrected. They set about doing something—and they succeeded. Each of them proved that even one person can start something big, that one person working alone can bring about important and needed changes. Even today we benefit from the ideas and the ideals of these brave, dedicated men and women.

JACOB BARSIMSON

The Right to Serve

17th Century

The Jews of New Amsterdam

On July 8, 1654, Jacob Barsimson left Holland on a ship called the *Peartree*. After a long, difficult voyage he arrived in the land of his dreams. He reached the New World on August 22 and landed in New Amsterdam. Other Jews had come through New Amsterdam as fur traders or peddlers, but Jacob was the first Jew to settle permanently in this Dutch colony in North America.

Like any other colonist who came at that time, Jacob was allotted a small hut outside the settlement. He cleared a piece of land, planted trees, and traded with the Indians. For a time he took a job as a laborer in order to earn some money.

About a month after Barsimson arrived twenty-three more Jews came to New Amsterdam. They were escaping from a place in Brazil called Recife, where the Portuguese had beaten the Dutch and driven out all the Jews. While

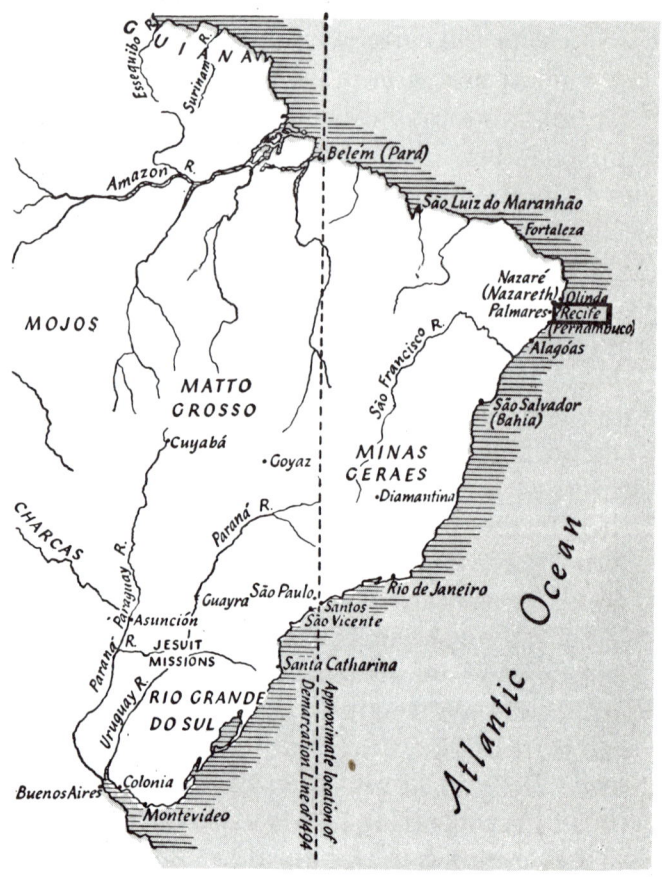

Map of the early settlements in Brazil. Recife is on the coast.

An artist's drawing of Recife.

at sea, sailing north, they had been attacked by pirates and robbed of all their belongings. Finally, they reached New Amsterdam.

Governor Stuyvesant Gets a Surprise

Peter Stuyvesant, the governor, was very angry when they tried to come ashore. He didn't want poor Jews to settle in his colony. He wrote a letter to Holland to complain about having to accept them in his new city. Much to his surprise a letter came back telling him that the Jews were to be made welcome in the colony. Peter Stuyvesant knew that he had to accept this decision, but he didn't like it one bit.

So the Jewish people were permitted to live among the original settlers. That didn't mean that they immediately achieved equality. It came slowly and with many setbacks.

The Fight for Equal Rights

Jacob Barsimson was not the kind of man to accept injustices without a fight. Once he was told to appear in court on a Saturday. Since he was an observant Jew, he refused to go because it was a violation of his Sabbath to transact any business on that day. After much deliberation the court authorities agreed that a Jew did not have to appear on Saturday. Jacob took a big chance when he decided to stand up for his rights. Had the ruling gone against him he could have been sent to prison. It could also have created problems for the other Jews who settled in New Amsterdam.

Jacob Barsimson was soon faced with another important decision. The men in the colony formed a home guard to protect the colony from pirates and hostile Indians. These men, with the approval of the governor, decided that Jews would not be allowed to join the guard.

A drawing of early New Amsterdam. Jews were among the first settlers in the Dutch colony.

Instead of serving in the guard, the Jewish men were required to pay a special tax. Jacob Barsimson rallied the Jews of New Amsterdam to meet and decide what to do about the tax. Many were willing to pay it. They had experienced the same kind of treatment in Europe. They didn't think they could oppose anything which the governor supported.

Only one of them was willing to join Jacob in fighting this injustice. Jacob Barsimson, with the help of his friend Asser Levy, decided to petition Governor Stuyvesant for the right to take part in the home guard or be exempt from paying the unfair tax. Their petition proclaimed: We are entitled to the same rights, privileges, and obligations as any other citizen in the community. We demand the same treatment as any other citizen. We insist on our right to serve our country.

A Victory with Important Effects

Governor Stuyvesant was angered by the demands and refused to accept the petition. Levy and Barsimson were not willing to be humiliated just because they were Jews. They continued their fight for two years. Finally, the governor accepted their petition and allowed Jews to serve in the home guard. When the British conquered New Amsterdam from the Dutch, they recognized and accepted the rights which Jacob Barsimson and Asser Levy had won for the Jews.

The victory which these men won made it possible for all Jews in America to have the right to bear arms. An important democratic principle was involved. Although not serving in an army isn't very serious in itself, being left out simply because one is a Jew makes it seem as if one person is not as good as his or her neighbor simply because of a religious difference. Barsimson and Levy insisted that people of all religions were entitled to the same rights and to equal treatment under the law. Ever since, this has been the American way.

Peter Stuyvesant marches at the head of his troops.

PUZZLE
FIND THE HIDDEN WORDS

Here is a list of words, names, and ideas which are found in the story. They also appear in the square below. In order to find them you will have to read in many directions:

Forward—from left to right;
Backward—from right to left:
Diagonal—in a slanted line from top to bottom
Up—from bottom to top; and
Down—from top to bottom.

As you find the words draw a line around them and cross the word off the list. For example: H O M E

JACOB
BARSIMSON
ASSER LEVY
PETER STUYVESANT
DUTCH
NEW AMSTERDAM
GUARD
EQUALITY
FREEDOM
JUSTICE
RIGHTS

```
A W N X J U S T I C E
M S E H A T D N L K N
H F W J T Q P A C N O
X O A G W Y J S D M U
J S M M O D E E R F O
A S S E R L E V Y L F
C X T B I E Q Y Z N B
O Z E A G Q D U T C H
B K R R H U D T K L Q
H S D S T A A S Y R T
P G A I S L J R X Y Z
G H M M M I G E D A P
T J S S P T Y T K W
H S Y O H Y L E B M R
A G K N E U G P L W Z
```

11

TEST YOURSELF

ARE THE FOLLOWING STATEMENTS TRUE OR FALSE?

1. Religious freedom is for the chosen people. T__ F__
2. All people living in the same community are entitled to the same rights. T__ F__
3. One person can change the way things are if his cause is fair. T__ F__
4. If a person is summoned to court he must appear even if that day is his Sabbath. T__ F__
5. Peter Stuyvesant welcomed all who wished to settle in New Amsterdam. T__ F__
6. Jacob Barsimson was not willing to be a second-class citizen in the New World. T__ F__
7. Barsimson was interested only in his own rights and privileges. T__ F__
8. Asser Levy did not want to serve in the home guard. T__ F__
9. The people of Holland had a special feeling for the Jews even in the New World. T__ F__
10. It is a limitation of a person's freedom if he or she is not allowed to do what other members of the same community are expected to do. T__ F__

QUOTATIONS

How do the following quotations relate to the story of Jacob Barsimson? Discuss them with your teacher.

"Proclaim liberty throughout the land unto all the inhabitants thereof."
BIBLE: Leviticus 25:10

"Fines are the same for all."
MISHNA: Ketubot 3:7

"To enforce one's rights when they are violated is never a legal wrong, and may often be a moral duty."
BENJAMIN CARDOZO

"Freedom is the joy of the world."
NACHMAN OF BRATISLAV

IDEAS OF VALUE

Think about this:

"Freedom is the joy of the world" (Nachman of Bratislav). That was the main reason Jacob Barsimson came to America. As an early settler he began to make others respect his Jewish observances. He refused to appear in court on a Saturday because to do so would have violated the Sabbath, his day of rest. He risked going to jail but felt that it was worth it if he could be assured of the freedom to practice his religion. He won his point and didn't have to go to court on the Sabbath. When Jews were told that they had to pay a tax instead of joining the home guard, he refused to accept that decision. "Fines are the same for all" (Mishna: *Ketubot* 3:7). Either all people could serve, regardless of their religion, or all people should pay the tax. He refused to accept the position of second-class citizen. It took two years of arguing but he finally won the right for Jews, as well as all others, to serve in the army.

You want to join a club. They agree to take you in as a member until they discover that you go to a different place of worship. Then they decide that you will be acceptable only if you pay a special fee. Does this in any way limit your freedom? What would you do? Why would you decide that way?

The dictionary defines prejudice as "irrational suspicion or hatred of a particular person or group." Jacob Barsimson was a religious Jew who faced prejudice because of his beliefs.

Governor Peter Stuyvesant refused to allow Jacob to join the home guard.

You have probably seen, read about, or felt examples of prejudice.

Write about examples of prejudice that you have seen in a real-life situation or on television or in a movie. You can include instances of discrimination, sexism, racism, or anti-Semitism.

URIAH LEVY

Fighting the United States Navy
1792–1862

A Boy Who Loved the Sea

In Talmudic times a Jewish child started his education at the age of three and chose a career by the age of ten. Following that tradition, Uriah Phillips Levy ran off to sea as a cabin boy at the age of ten. That was in the year 1802. He learned quickly, and by the age of twenty he had been given command of the sloop *George Washington*.

Uriah's men mutinied, however, and put him ashore on a deserted island. At that time Britain was at war with France. A British ship found Uriah, but after the British rescued him, they tried to force him to serve in their navy. No matter how they tried to trick him or punish him, he refused to sign on as a British seaman. At the first port he overpowered his guard and ran away.

A Hero of the War of 1812

Uriah made his way back to America just after the War of 1812 began between Britain and the United States. He was assigned to the *Argus* as assistant sailing master. The *Argus* sank or captured

A painting of the brig *Argus*, which destroyed several million dollars worth of English shipping during the War of 1812.

15

twenty-one British ships. The last sloop it captured was still seaworthy.

Since the United States was badly in need of ships, Uriah Phillips Levy was put in charge of taking the captured vessel back to Philadelphia. On the way he engaged a British warship in battle and his ship was very badly damaged. Levy was captured and spent the rest of the war in a London jail.

A Career in the Navy

After the war, in 1816, Levy was returned to the United States. Because of his bravery he was commissioned a lieutenant in the regular Navy. Most of the other officers were not happy about this. They were unwilling to accept someone who had started out as a cabin boy instead of attending the Naval Academy—especially when the man in question was a Jew.

Being Jewish was a very important part of Uriah Levy's life. Once he heard another officer make an anti-Semitic remark. He was so angry that he challenged the man to a duel. When the time came, he figured, he would only scare his opponent by firing in his direction. He really didn't want to kill his opponent, but when he realized the man was trying to hit him, he had to shoot him. Levy was court-martialed and dismissed from the Navy. In fact, he was court-martialed six times, and each time he was cleared and was allowed to return to service.

Uriah Levy was not promoted for twenty years. After he proved himself a great hero by putting an end to piracy in the Caribbean Sea, the government was forced to promote him. He was made a commander. Then, in 1844, he was made a captain after he distinguished himself by stopping illegal slave traffic in Honduras Bay. After this assignment there never seemed to be any more jobs for Uriah Levy. The Navy was trying to get him to resign.

Uriah Levy was not willing to give in to this kind of pressure. Instead he decided to investigate a terrible evil. It was the custom and tradition of the sea that the captain was in absolute control of the men on his ship. If he ordered them to risk their lives they had no choice but to do so. If he wanted to feed them very little food or give them no water to drink, he could do so. If they refused to obey his commands, or if they complained about their treatment, the captain could order any kind of punishment he wanted. The men were treated like beasts on many ships. Sometimes they were beaten to death.

Uriah P. Levy

Uriah Phillips Levy resented the loss of human dignity among the seamen. He decided that he had to do something to correct the situation. He went to Washington and told some Congressmen about the cruel and inhuman punishments that were going on in the Navy. He convinced them that something had to be done.

Captain Uriah Phillips Levy showing the cat-o-nine-tails to Washington legislators during his campaign to stop flogging in the U.S. Navy. This painting hangs in the Mariners' Museum in Newport News, Virginia.

A report on the trial of Commander Uriah P. Levy.

Uriah Levy on Trial

In 1850, thanks to Uriah Levy's efforts, Congress abolished corporal punishment in the Navy. This was truly a great achievement toward furthering the rights of people in a free, democratic country. Not too many of Uriah's fellow officers thought so, however. In 1855 he was discharged from the Navy. Aware that he was being forced out of the service because of his action against corporal punishment, and because he was Jewish, Uriah demanded publicly that his case be reviewed by a Court of Enquiry.

Seven captains of the United States Navy were selected to hear his case. Uriah Phillips Levy was his own spokesman. He had his naval record read aloud. His heroism was clearly stated. Since the United States Congress had passed a law prohibiting corporal punishment, he said, he didn't have to make excuses for working for that change. At last came the big question. How was it that he had received so few assignments as a captain? In answer to this Uriah looked straight at the seven men and began to tell the story of his life in the Navy. He told how he had started as a cabin boy and gained his promotions by hard work. He also told them about the abuses and slurs against him because he was Jewish. After this detailed defense he sat down.

The jury of his peers did not even leave the room to take a vote. They immediately recommended his reinstatement to active duty as a captain in the United States Navy. Two years later Uriah Levy was promoted to the rank of commodore, the highest rank of all at that time.

So much did Uriah Levy love his country, in spite of the hardships he was forced to undergo, that he used his own money to restore Monticello, the home of Thomas Jefferson, a man he admired greatly. When Uriah died, in 1862, he left the Federal Government $300,000. And to every man and woman who has ever joined the Navy he left the assurance of just and humane treatment.

In 1943, to show its appreciation for this determined, honorable man who was so concerned with justice on land and at sea, the U.S. government named a destroyer-escort the U.S.S. *Levy*. Then, in 1959, in Norfolk, Virginia, the first permanent Jewish Naval Chapel was named the Commodore Levy Chapel.

Thomas Jefferson's home in Monticello. Levy purchased and restored the home and gave it to the United States as a national memorial.

PUZZLE

By using the letter instead of the number you will be able to figure out what Uriah Phillips Levy contributed to the greatness of this country even though he was only one person.

For example: 26 represents Z

8 5   23 15 21 12 4   14 15 20

1 3 3 5 16 20   9 14 10 21 19 20 9 3 5

6 15 18   8 9 13 19 5 12 6   15 18

1 14 25 15 14 5   5 12 19 5.

TEST YOURSELF

Here are some of the things which made Uriah Phillips Levy a very special person.

Can you match the words and ideas in column A with those in column B?

A	B
1. ten years old	1943
2. duel	restored and given to the people of the United States
3. corporal punishment	six times
4. court-martial	cabin boy
5. promotion	found Uriah Levy worthy of serving in the Navy
6. Monticello	Commodore Levy Chapel
7. U.S.S. *Levy*	hard work
8. 1959	lobbied to get law passed against
9. jury of his peers	anti-Semitic remark

QUOTATIONS

How do the following quotations relate to the story of Uriah Phillips Levy?

Discuss them with your teacher.

"Anti-Semitism is not to be overcome by getting people to forget us, but to know us."

MEYER LEVIN, In Search

"Who is a hero? He who turns an enemy into a friend."

ABOT DE RABBI NATHAN 23

"Leave not a stain on your honor."

APOCRYPHA: Ecclesiasticus 33:22

"Never act insolently or tyrannically in your treatment of offenders."

APOCRYPHA: Aristeas 191

IDEAS OF VALUE

Think about this:

Uriah Phillips Levy rose from cabin boy to become an officer in the United States Navy. While in command he put an end to piracy in the Caribbean Sea and stopped slave traffic in Honduras Bay. Each time he was promoted. Then, suddenly, his progress stopped. He was court-martialed and dismissed from the Navy six times because he stood up for justice and against anti-Semitism.

"Anti-Semitism is not to be overcome by getting people to forget us, but to know us" (Meyer Levin, *In Search*).

Then Levy decided to spend his time working against the system which gave the captain of a ship total power over his men. He finally succeeded in having corporal punishment outlawed in the United States Navy. The Navy tried to get him to resign. He demanded a public hearing and got it. He turned out to be a hero. "Who is a hero? He who turns an enemy into a friend" (*Abot de R. Nathan*, chap. 23). He finally was able to make his fellow officers understand what it was like for a Jewish person to rise from cabin boy to officer. Again, he was cleared of all charges and given a promotion.

You are the captain of a volleyball team. Some of the players want you to get rid of another person on the team. That person is as good a player as any of the others but she comes from a different neighborhood.
What would your answer be? Why did you decide on it? When would you give in to the pressure, and when would you fight back?

Uriah Phillips Levy became a commodore in the United States Navy. All his life he had to fight the anti-Semitism of his fellow officers.

Have you ever been involved in a situation where you had to fight for your rights as a Jew or as a person? Tell about it.

Which freedom would you be willing to give up without a fight?
I would willingly give up the right to _____.

What freedom would you fight for?
I would be willing to fight for _____.
I would fight for this right because _____.

What is your definition of freedom?

ERNESTINE ROSE

The Lady with the Petitions
1810–1892

A Girl Who Knew What She Wanted

It all started when she was very young. The custom in her village in Poland allowed only boys to study the Bible in Hebrew. That made Ernestine very angry. She felt it was her right to study if she wanted to. So her father, who was a respected rabbi, finally gave in and hired a tutor for her. The tutor didn't last very long because Ernestine had a way of asking questions that he could not, or would not, answer. She wanted to know how the universe was formed. She wanted to know how things became evil. She wanted to know why it was a sin to do this or that. Nobody wanted to answer these questions for her.

When Ernestine was about sixteen her mother died. Her father thought it was time for his daughter to be married, or, at least, engaged. In the year 1826 most young women were promised in marriage at a very early age. What's more, they were usually promised to men chosen by their fathers. The rabbi made what he considered a good match for Ernestine and then he told her about it. She was very upset and refused to accept the arrangement. Even though her father had already promised the man her inheritance from her mother, she still would not agree to the marriage. She pleaded with her father. She pleaded with the man. Neither would release her from the promise. She insisted that she did not love the man and would not marry him.

A Polish Jew and his wife.

Ernestine's Day in Court

Usually, when Jewish people in the town had a quarrel with each other, they went to the rabbi for a solution to the problem. This time, Ernestine thought, that was impossible since her father was a party to the quarrel. She decided to sue her father in the Polish court. This was unheard of for three reasons. Girls did not sue for the right to marry or not to marry, girls did not sue their own fathers, and girls did not try their own cases in court. But that is exactly what Ernestine did.

She hired a carriage and a driver to take her to the town where she would present her case. More than a week went by before it was her turn. While waiting Ernestine sat in the courtroom every day to learn the procedure. Even though she was very nervous she stated her case. She told the judge that she didn't think it was fair to have to marry a man she didn't love. She also didn't think it fair for the man to keep her inheritance just because she would not keep a contract which she had no part in making. The judge was impressed. When Ernestine left the court she had a paper which restored her inheritance and freed her from the promise that her father made for her. She felt very good about the victory for justice she had won. On her way home she decided to turn the money over to her father whom she really loved very dearly.

Ernestine Meets the King

Soon after this experience Ernestine decided that she would like to see how people lived in other parts of the world. She didn't know where she wanted to settle for the rest of her life, but she knew that Poland wasn't a good place for Jews.

Ernestine Rose

She took just enough money from her father to pay for a trip to Berlin. When she arrived in Germany she was surprised to learn that Jews were not welcome. They were permitted to stay only a short time and were not allowed to earn any money while they were there. This struck her as very unjust. Having had such a successful experience with a Polish court, she decided to try to get some justice in Germany as well. She wrote a letter to the king asking for permission to come to see him.

After a few days Ernestine received an invitation to the royal court. She was very excited but a little bit frightened. When the time came for her appearance she gathered her courage and stated her case very simply. She was there to plead for justice, she said. As a Jewess she felt that the law not allowing Jews freedom to live and work where they wanted was wrong and unfair.

A Women's Rights meeting. Ernestine is the third woman from the right in the front row.

The king was very impressed by her petition. While he would not agree to change the laws, he allowed Ernestine to stay in Germany as long as she wanted and to earn money any way she was able. Once again her petition in a just cause won.

The Fight for Women's Rights

As Ernestine traveled from country to country she saw how difficult it was for women and children. They had no rights and no freedoms. They belonged either to their fathers or to their husbands. If a man wanted to, he could send his six- or seven-year-old children to work in factories and coal mines. Whatever they earned was given to the father to use as he wished. The same was true with women. A married woman had no right to own property. She could neither sue nor be sued in court. And worst of all, her earnings and her children belonged to her husband.

This was true in European countries and also in the United States, as Ernestine discovered when she came to this country with her husband, William Rose. Ernestine and William hoped to enjoy freedom and democracy in the new world. What they found was not what they expected. Ernestine could not vote, but she had to pay taxes to the government which deprived her of this right. She was not willing to accept this situation.

In 1836 a bill dealing with the property rights of married women was introduced in the New York State Legislature. Ernestine Rose decided to help get the bill passed by circulating a petition. All she had to do, she thought, was go from house to house and ask the women to sign. She would send hundreds and hundreds of signatures to Albany, the capital, and the bill would be passed.

Oh, was she mistaken. The women would not sign the petition. They were afraid their husbands might find out. At the end of five months Ernestine had exactly five signatures. These she sent off to Albany. No one paid any attention to them, and another year went by without any new rights being granted to women.

Each year Ernestine tried again, and each year she made more headway with her petition. She made speeches where-ever she could gather an audience. Soon she was the most well known woman lecturer for freedom and democratic rights. She also spoke out against slavery, organizing people and writing petitions for this cause as well.

Victory at Last

In March 1860, the legislature passed a law making women equal to their husbands. Women now could own property and had equal rights with their husbands concerning the care of their children. In fact, women had everything except the right to vote.

Ernestine Rose continued her fight for justice and equality throughout her life. She did not, however, live long enough to see women allowed to vote and run for public office. Ernestine Rose died in 1892. Women were not given the vote until 1920.

The laws we have today which give equality to minorities are in great measure due to the tireless, hard work of this daughter of a Polish rabbi who came to America to seek freedom.

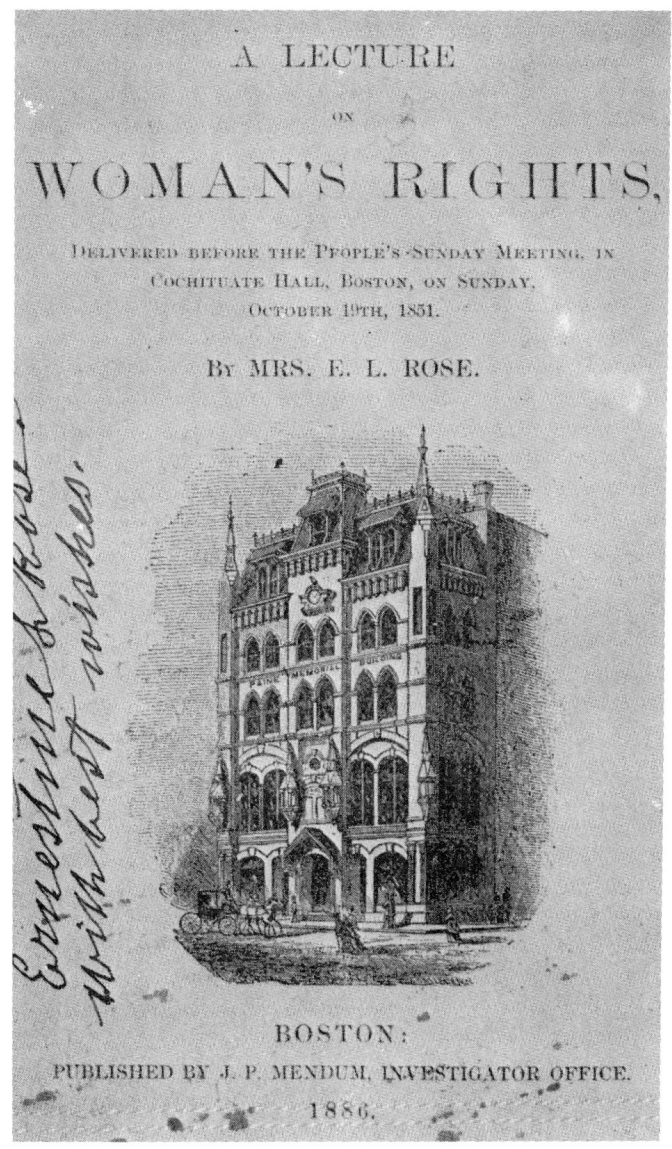

A copy of a speech delivered by Ernestine Rose in 1851. This pamphlet was the personal property of Susan B. Anthony.

TEST YOURSELF

Complete the following sentences with the words found on the list below.

1. Ernestine Rose was one of the first _____.
2. Making _____ was one of her talents.
3. She was against the oppression of _____ and _____.
4. She was also against _____.
5. One of her most powerful weapons was the signatures on _____.
6. Ernestine's father was a _____ in Poland.
7. Her earliest rebellion was against her father because he tried to arrange her _____.
8. She felt that _____ were entitled to study Torah.
9. Her husband agreed with her _____.

RABBI
IDEAS
SLAVERY
PETITIONS
WOMEN'S-LIBBERS
WOMEN AND CHILDREN
SPEECHES
MARRIAGE
GIRLS

QUOTATIONS

How do the following quotations relate to the story of Ernestine Rose?

Discuss them with your teacher.

"A daughter is a treasure—and a cause of sleeplessness."
APOCRYPHA: Ecclesiasticus 42:9

"A person's father is his king."
PIRKE DE RABBI ELIEZER

"If I do not acquire ideals in my youth, when will I?"
MAIMONIDES

"The person who persists in knocking will succeed in entering."
MOSES IBN EZRA, Shirat Yisrael

"All men, women, and children met at the foot of Mount Sinai. This in itself is a proclamation of equality."
ISAAC MAYER WISE, Outlines of Judaism

PUZZLE

To solve this word puzzle you must write the words listed in their correct places. One word is included to start you off. Now find the word with the proper number of letters that fits with this word. For example: find a word that starts with E and has five letters. Write this word under the E in *petition*. Cross off each word on the list as you use it so you won't repeat it.

<u>2 Letters</u>
in

<u>3 Letters</u>
saw
few
new
sit
inn
alp

<u>4 Letters</u>
sign
stir
will

<u>5 Letters</u>
equal
onset
women
sivan

<u>6 Letters</u>
rights

<u>8 Letters</u>
~~petition~~

IDEAS OF VALUE

Think about this:

Long before anyone had thought of the sit-in, Ernestine Rose thought of the speak-out. She spoke out when she wanted to study the Bible and girls were not allowed to. She spoke out against discrimination when she learned that Jews could only remain in Germany for a limited time. She spoke out against the practice of the woman and her children belonging to her husband like so much property. She spoke out against child labor and slavery. But words were not enough. She knew that "The person who persists in knocking will succeed in entering" (Moses ibn Ezra, *Shirat Yisrael*). She set about to correct these injustices and was not easily discouraged. She made speeches and carried petitions wherever she went. No matter how tired she was, she continued with her speak-out program. "The need for speech and work is greater than the need for silence and rest" (Moses ibn Ezra, *Shirat Yisrael*). In many of these matters she was able to correct the evils and get justice for her causes.

There is very little difference between being persistent (going after what you want) and being a pest. Under what conditions would you be willing to risk being called a pest if you were persistent?

Ernestine Rose spent her life speaking out. She spoke out for the rights of children and women and against slavery. No doubt there have been many times when you wanted to speak out.

Draw or write about the times that you wished to speak out.

A time I spoke out and was glad . . .

A time I spoke out and learned something new . . .

A time I spoke out and was sad . . .

A time I spoke out and felt like an idiot . . .

A time I wanted to speak out and was scared . . .

JOSEPH GOLDBERGER

An Immigrant Makes His Mark

1874-1929

Joseph Goldberger's Early Life

In 1880 a Jewish family came to America from Eastern Europe. Its youngest member was a six-year-old boy named Joseph. Samuel Goldberger, the boy's father, opened a small grocery store, and the family lived in the rooms behind it. Every member of the family worked to contribute to the support of the household. Although Joseph was the youngest, he ran errands, shined shoes, and did whatever he could to earn a few pennies each day after school.

Joseph studied very hard to learn the new language and all he could about his new country. Each Sabbath, the only day the family didn't work, he reported all that he had learned during the week.

Joseph Becomes a Doctor

As Joseph grew older, it was easy to see that he was a very good student. His brother and sisters saved every penny they could in order to make it possible for him to go to college. At first he planned to be an engineer. Later he changed his mind and decided to become a doctor. He intended to devote his life to medicine and the prevention of disease.

Joseph Goldberger graduated from Bellevue Medical College in 1895. He went into private practice for a few years, but he was not satisfied with trying to cure diseases. He wanted to prevent illnesses before they started.

Joseph Goldberger

A U.S. Public Health scientist at work in a medical laboratory.

A New Way of Studying Diseases

In 1899, when the United States government established a Public Health Service, Joseph Goldberger was appointed Assistant Surgeon. He moved to Washington, D.C., where laboratories with the most up-to-date equipment were available to him. He also had an office where, if he wished, he could sit and think about health problems. That was not for him. He felt that the way to study a medical problem was to go to the scene and investigate.

In keeping with this theory Joseph Goldberger went to Tampico and Vera Cruz, in Mexico, to help discover the cause, and later the cure, for typhus and yellow fever. These were very contagious diseases and he became ill with typhus. He was lucky enough to recover and was sent back to Washington. He still felt that the only way to find solutions was to go to where the problems were. He proved his point when it took him only two days to isolate the cause of an ailment called "straw itch," a serious problem for sailors. At sea the men slept on straw mattresses, and very tiny, almost invisible insects called mites infested the beds. Once they got rid of the mites, the itch went too. This was only a small thing, but it prevented a great many people from being sick and uncomfortable.

Pellagra: A Mysterious Disease

In 1914 Joseph Goldberger went to the southern part of the United States to investigate a disease called pellagra. This disease had been around for a long time and had caused misery and death to a great many poor people. Those who had pellagra were unable to work; they got tired very quickly; they began to show red, blotchy skin rashes; and before long they became insane and died. Because pellagra often affected people living at close quarters, it was thought to be contagious or infectious. In other words, doctors thought that people caught pellagra from one another.

Using his special approach to medical problems, Dr. Goldberger went to the scene of the trouble. He observed and asked questions. He visited orphans' homes and prisons and other places where poor people lived in crowded conditions. He soon noticed something important. People who got pellagra ate different foods from those who remained healthy. Joseph Goldberger investigated further and carefully followed up every clue. He became convinced that pellagra was caused by a poor diet, and not by germs. Other doctors would not accept his theory.

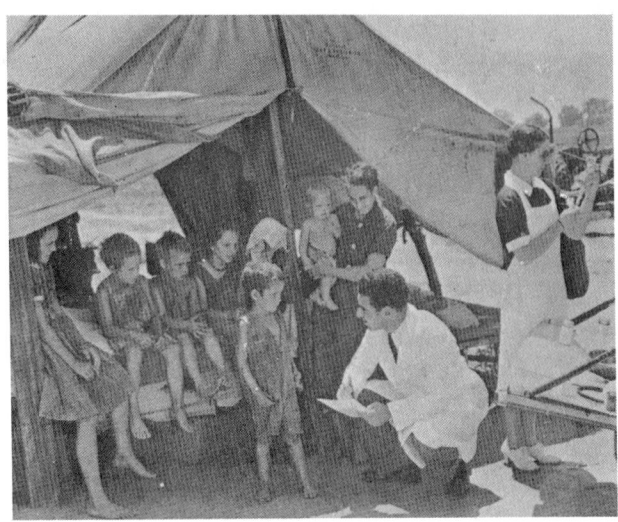

A U.S. Public Health medical team at work in the field.

Joseph Goldberger Proves His Theory

In order to get proof, Joseph Goldberger arranged for the government to provide a group of orphan children with a balanced diet that included fresh vegetables, meat, and milk. Soon the disease disappeared and the children were healthy again. Other medical authorities were still not ready to accept the exciting discovery. They wanted even more proof.

Next Joseph Goldberger went to a prison farm in Mississippi and asked the inmates to help him with an experiment. They would be set free if they would help him prove that food made the difference. At first the men resisted. They were afraid they might die if Dr. Goldberger was wrong. They agreed when he appealed to them to be heroes of science.

For six months the prisoners were housed in very sanitary conditions but were fed the normal diet of the poor. They gradually became ill with all the symptoms of pellagra. Once their diet was improved they became well again. Other scientists were still skeptical. They wanted more proof. They still believed that the disease was passed from one person to another.

This time Dr. Goldberger had to do something drastic. He injected blood from people who were ill into his assistant and himself. They watched and waited for symptoms to appear. After two weeks, when nothing happened, they tried some other experiments on themselves. They still did not contract the sickness. Finally, after all these experiments, the other doctors began to agree that Dr. Goldberger was correct. But Joseph Goldberger wasn't satisfied with finding the cause of the disease. He wanted to prevent the disease from ever occurring again. Knowing that proper food could prevent pellagra, he also worked on a scheme that enabled poor people to grow the foods they needed.

During all the years that pellagra was a health problem, nobody bothered to study how the affected people lived. Dr. Joseph Goldberger, by going to the scene of the problem, found the clues which led to the solution. He saw that people were suffering and wanted to help. His persistence led to the elimination of a dreaded sickness.

TEST YOURSELF

After you have read the story, complete the following sentences.

1. The illness for which Dr. Goldberger found a cure is _____.
2. Important changes take place because of _____.
3. In a Jewish family _____ is so important that every member will work hard for it.
4. Among the most important foods for people to eat are _____.
5. Goldberger's discovery helped people all over the _____.
6. Being observant can help one find the _____ to a problem.

PUZZLE

CAN YOU BREAK THE CODE?

The sentence below is spelled out in a different arrangement of letters in the alphabet than you are accustomed to. Can you figure out the new order? Here is a hint for you. "A = Z"

LMV KVIHLM XZM WL

HLNVGSRMT DSRXS DROO

SVOK NZMB LGSVIH.

QUOTATIONS

How do the following quotations relate to the story of Dr. Joseph Goldberger?

Discuss them with your teacher.

"Poverty in the home is worse than fifty plagues."
TALMUD: *Baba Bathra* 116a

"Wisdom without action is like a tree without fruit."
JOSEPH KIMHI, *Shekel Hakodesh* 12c

"If one man says, 'You're a donkey,' don't mind; if two say so, be worried; if three say so, get a saddle."
MIDRASH: *Genesis Rabbah* 45:10

IDEAS OF VALUE

Think about this:

As early as the thirteenth century, in a book called *Sefer Hasidim*, we learn: "Who is a good physician? He who can prevent disease." Joseph Goldberger became a doctor and went into private practice. After a short time he decided that what he really wanted was to prevent disease, not only to cure it. He joined the United States Public Health Service. There, he didn't earn as much money, but he had the chance to serve humanity. He helped find cures for typhus and yellow fever. He also helped the Navy by finding the cause and cure of "straw itch." His greatest achievement was finding the cause and cure of pellagra. While doing this he was able to teach poor people what food to grow to avoid future illness. He devoted his life and his skill to making life a little better for a great many people.

Dr. Goldberger could be called an altruist—someone who does something for others without expecting payment or a reward. How can you, as a young person, be an altruist? When is being an altruist good, and when is it not?

Joseph Goldberger left private medical practice to work for the United States Public Health Service.

There he helped find cures for many diseases. He devoted his time to making life more comfortable and healthier for many people.

Think of some things you have done in your life.

Write about your biggest success.

Write about your biggest failure.

Write about something you wish you had never done.

Write about something you would like to do to help someone or some institution.

NATHAN STRAUS

The Great Giver
1848–1931

The Building of a Business Empire

Have you ever wondered where people who become philanthropists get the money that they give away? Sometimes they inherit it from their parents. Sometimes they invent something which makes them very rich. Sometimes they discover gold or oil. Sometimes they earn fortunes by their own ingenuity and hard work.

Nathan Straus was one of those who worked hard and made a fortune.

He was born in Bavaria and was brought to America when he was six years old. His father, Lazarus Straus, was a peddler and storekeeper in Georgia. That is where Nathan, as a small boy, used to dream about how nice it would be to save somebody's life. The family lived in the South until after the Civil War. In 1866 they moved to New York.

Once they settled there, Lazarus Straus went into business selling dishes and glassware. Nathan was sent to college so that he could be useful in the family business. As part of his work for the family he became a salesman. He went to the big stores to try to interest them in the merchandise the family was selling.

Nathan Straus

One of the big stores he visited was R. H. Macy and Company. He went there with two plates under his arm. These were the samples he carried to show the kind of dishes he was selling. Nathan was such a good salesman that he didn't simply interest Mr. Macy in the product. He also arranged to rent the entire basement of the store. This would be a special dish and glassware department selling only the Straus products. When Nathan was twenty-six years old he and his brother became partners in R. H. Macy and Company. Two years later they bought the entire business. That was the beginning of the growth of department stores as we know them today.

A few years later they bought another department store. This one was in Brooklyn, New York. It was called Abraham and Straus. In this way Nathan Straus became one of the wealthiest businessmen in the world.

The Battle for Safe Milk

Nathan Straus was not really anxious to keep on making money. He wanted to do something worthwhile with what he had. He began to give money to different charities and projects. He helped Henrietta Szold in her work in Palestine. His

A delivery truck which transported pasteurized milk.

greatest concern, however, was for the health and welfare of poor babies.

Nathan Straus and his family lived on a farm. They raised their own livestock and drank the milk from their own cows. When one of their cows died of tuberculosis, Nathan Straus realized the great danger to which city children were exposed. There was no such thing as inspection of farms or testing of the milk supply to be sure that it was pure. In the city, many babies were dying and no cause could be found. He began to suspect that spoiled milk might be the reason.

Nathan Straus started a one-man campaign to investigate dairy farms. What he found shocked him. The barns were dirty. No care was taken to be sure that the milk was kept fresh and clean. Sometimes sick cows were not separated from healthy ones. Nathan Straus felt that sick cows could pass their ailments on to humans. Something had to be done to protect the babies who were drinking this milk which could be contaminated so easily.

A workshop at the Nathan Straus Foundation, Jerusalem.

In 1892 Nathan Straus went to a conference in Brussels, Belgium. At this meeting Louis Pasteur demonstrated his new method of treating milk, which was called pasteurization. He showed that any germs in the milk treated by his new method would be absolutely harmless. Nathan Straus was impressed by what he saw and learned. He decided to introduce the new process at home.

He set up laboratories all over New York City where milk could be tested and treated. Then he started the Straus Milk Fund, which distributed pasteurized milk from his own labs to the poor. He charged much less than the dairies did. In the summer, when it was especially important to be careful about the quality of milk, he gave it away to the poor at no cost at all.

In the meantime he was campaigning for adequate milk inspection throughout the State of New York. Other businessmen fought his proposals. It would cost them more if they had to inspect the milk and discard any that was not up to standard. Straus fought on. After twenty

A newspaper drawing of a Nathan Straus coal depot.

years he was able to close his private pasteurization plants, for by then, New York, as well as every other state, had passed laws that required the proper treatment and inspection of milk.

Nathan Straus saved the lives of many thousands of babies because of his insistence that pure milk was important to their health and growth.

Helping the Poor

In 1892 there was widespread unemployment in the United States. That winter was a very cold one. A great many poor people couldn't afford to buy coal to heat their homes. This led to much sickness and despair. Nathan Straus saw that the people needed help. They wanted to work but there were very few jobs available. Once again, he used his personal wealth to make life a little easier for those who were in need. He didn't want them to feel that they were taking charity, but he did want them to have the coal they needed. He arranged for baskets of coal to be sold for five cents each. Those who needed the fuel were able to get it and still keep their self-respect. Over one million baskets were distributed that year.

Hot coffee and a roll for one penny. Scene at Nathan Straus milk station, winter of 1914–1915.

Nathan Straus tuberculosis hospital in Lakewood, New Jersey.

The next year conditions were not better. Jobs still were not available and money was very scarce. Nathan Straus provided food, coal, and places to sleep for those who were in need. In 1914 and 1915 Straus served meals for one cent in his milk stations. The nickname he earned from those who received his gifts was "The Great Giver."

Helping Israel

Nathan Straus's philosophy included making it possible for others to earn a living. In Palestine he started a factory which made mother-of-pearl buttons. Because there was work, the people didn't need to accept charity. He gave about two-thirds of all his money to projects in the land of Israel.

The Israelis wanted to show how grateful they were for all Nathan Straus did to help develop the land of Israel. When he was eighty years old, Natanya, a colony near Tel Aviv, was established in his honor.

At the age of eighty-three the Grand Old Man of American Jewry died. His life was spent doing what he felt was helpful to others. He earned a great deal of wealth and he spent it in a great manner. His childhood dream of saving lives was achieved many times in his milk centers, in his help to the poor during times of crisis, and in his great interest in the development of Israel.

Soup kitchen at the Nathan Straus Foundation, Jerusalem.

TEST YOURSELF

In the following sentences underline the correct phrase.

1. Nathan Straus made a lot of money by (a) discovering gold, (b) working hard, (c) inventing the radio.
2. Even as a small child he wanted to (a) save a life, (b) become President, (c) be a fireman.
3. He and his brother bought (a) airplanes, (b) race horses, (c) department stores.
4. Straus realized the importance of sanitary conditions in (a) movies, (b) farms, (c) roads.
5. Pasteur and his milk process had (a) little effect, (b) great effect, (c) no effect on Nathan Straus.
6. During a depression Nathan Straus sold baskets of coal for (a) $5, (b) 5 cents, (c) $2.50.
7. In the summertime at his milk stations he charged (a) 25 cents, (b) 10 cents, (c) nothing.
8. He started a button factory in Israel so (a) he could get richer, (b) people could earn money, (c) he could start a new fashion.
9. There is a colony in (a) Japan, (b) United States, (c) Israel named in his honor.
10. Department stores began to develop when Straus bought (a) markets, (b) R. H. Macy and Company, (c) 5 and 10 cents stores.

PUZZLE

The following words appeared in the story of Nathan Straus . If you have trouble reading the words try looking at them in a mirror.

1. PASTEURIZE
2. NATANYA
3. MILK
4. COAL
5. BUTTONS
6. GENEROUS
7. DISHES

QUOTATIONS

How do the following quotations relate to the story of Nathan Straus?

Discuss them with your teacher.

"Nobody is ever impoverished through the giving of charity."
MAIMONIDES

"Love, cherish, and esteem the children of other people."
BENJAMIN DISRAELI

"The greatest charity is to enable the poor to earn a living."
TALMUD: Shabbat 63a

"A torch is not diminished though it kindles a million candles, so he will not lose who gives to a good cause."
MIDRASH: Exodus Rabbah 30:3

"Not to teach your son to work is like teaching him to steal."
TALMUD: Kiddushin 29a

"No labor, no matter how humble, dishonors a person."
TALMUD: Nedarim 49b

IDEAS OF VALUE

Think about this:

Nathan Straus worked hard. He was a businessman who earned a great deal of money. Once he had it, he decided to use it for good purposes. "Nobody is ever impoverished through the giving of charity" (Maimonides, *Yad: Matnot Aniyim*). He was concerned with the health and welfare of poor babies. He established a milk fund to be sure that they had enough good-quality milk. During economic hard times he helped provide coal, food, and shelter to those who were in need. He also tried to make it possible for people to earn money rather than take charity. "The greatest charity is to enable the poor to earn a living" (Talmud: *Shabbat* 63a).

A person doesn't have to be rich to give charity. "Even a poor man, a subject of charity, should give charity" (Talmud: Gittin 7b). If you were going to give charity, how would you decide to whom to give your money?

Nathan Straus was a very wealthy man. He spent his money and most of his life helping poor people. He established a milk fund and helped provide food and shelter for those in need.

Suppose you were an extremely wealthy person and had lots and lots of money.

How could you help people less fortunate than yourself?

What kind of project would you start?

How would you go about organizing the project?

LILLIAN WALD

The Superwoman of Henry Street

A Rich Girl Helps the Poor 1867–1940

Most stories about heroes and heroines start with people who are poor and work their way to riches. This is the story of a woman who was born wealthy but chose to live among the poor. Lillian Wald's parents, Max and Minnie, were rich. They expected her to lead a life of leisure and pleasure. They thought she should go to parties, meet nice young men, and marry one of them. Then she could live a comfortable life and raise several children.

Lillian had other ideas. When she was sixteen and had learned as much as she could at the private school she was attending, she applied for admission to Vassar College. Her grades were fine but the dean felt she was too young. She was asked to apply again in a couple of years. Lillian was very disappointed.

However, it wasn't too long before Lillian Wald found what she felt would be a worthwhile way to spend her life. When her sister became ill a nurse was called in. After watching how helpful the nurse was, Lillian decided that becoming a nurse would enable her to be useful and independent. She could use her talents and help others. She went to nursing school. The more she saw while she was studying, the more she realized how much there was to be done for the poor people.

Lillian Wald in a nurse's uniform.

The new immigrants lived in great poverty and diseases spread quickly. This Jew is observing the Sabbath in his cellar home.

A Nurse on the Lower East Side

Many new immigrants to this country were settling on the Lower East Side of New York. They were taken in by relatives already there, or they rented space in other people's apartments. Living quarters became very crowded. As they became more crowded they became dirtier. The combination of too many people and poor facilities caused disease to spread very quickly in these houses.

One of Lillian Wald's first experiences on the Lower East Side influenced most of her future life. She met a hideous-looking little boy on the street. When she asked him why he wasn't in school, he told her that the teacher kept sending him home. When Lillian looked closer she saw that he had a bad rash. She knew it could be cleared up easily with proper treatment. She took the boy to his house, applied some medicine, and showed his mother how to take care of him. In a short time the boy looked fine and the teacher allowed him to stay in school.

Nurse Wald decided that in order to be really useful she had to move to the neighborhood. The people would no longer consider her an outsider. They would get to know and trust her. First Lillian and a friend moved into an apartment. Later, they set up the Henry Street Settlement House, which soon became world-famous for its work and programs.

School Nurses and Public Health Nurses

But these weren't the only results of Lillian's experience with the boy. She realized that many children were kept out of school because their parents didn't know how to cure their illnesses. Other children were coming to school with diseases that could infect their classmates. Lillian Wald concluded that the school system should provide nurses to spot children with illnesses and send them home. Lillian took her idea to the school board and then to the mayor. It took a while to convince them, but thanks to Lillian's stubborn nature, New York City finally got its school nurses.

Lillian and her friend also began to visit houses where there were no children, but many times they were viewed with suspicion. The poor people were embarrassed when the nurses came to the door because the whole neighborhood would know they were taking charity. Lillian decided that she and her friend needed credentials from the city government. That would make them officials and they could even charge a fee. Whatever the family could afford, no matter how little, would be acceptable. If people were paying, they wouldn't be ashamed to accept help. After much persuasion Lillian and her friend finally got badges, and thus began the new idea of public health nurses.

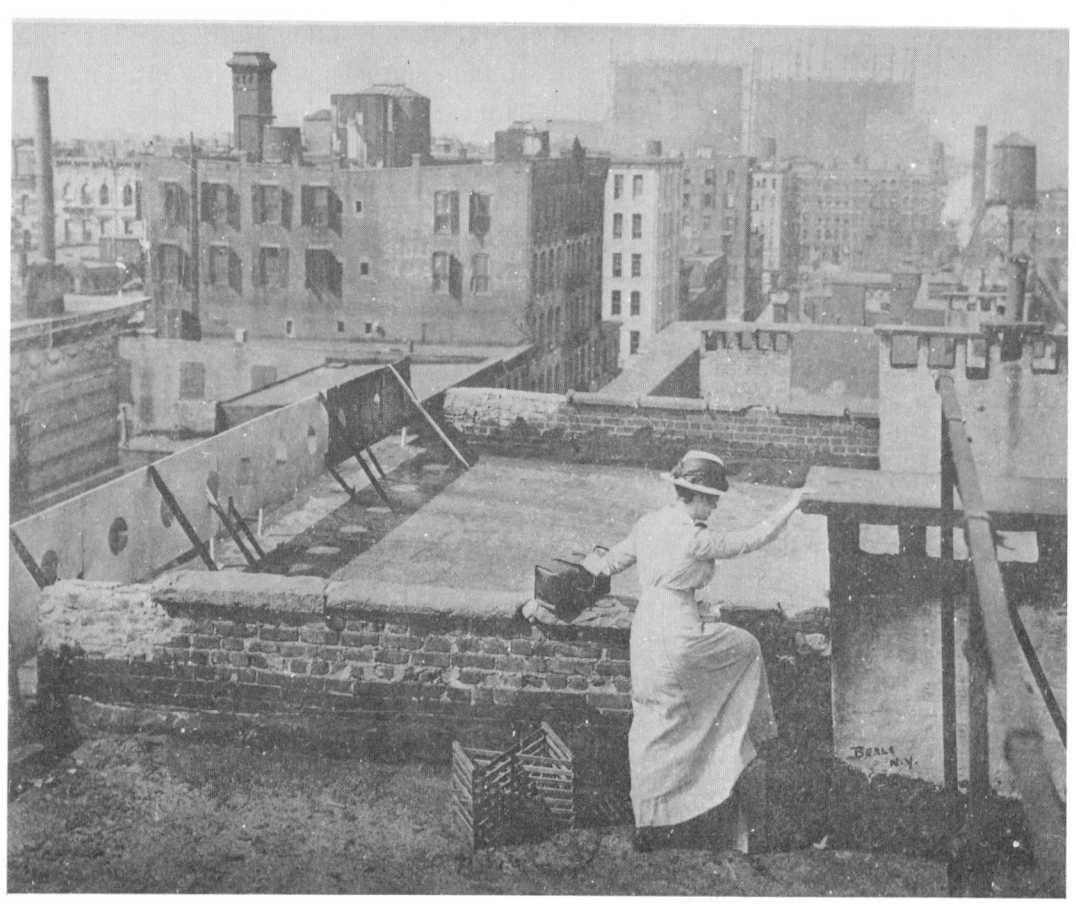

A public health nurse climbs over rooftops to visit her patients.

The Henry Street Settlement House

Money was needed for this project as well as for other ideas Lillian Wald wanted to put into operation at the Henry Street House. She called upon her wealthy German-Jewish friends who had come to New York many years earlier. One of them was Jacob Schiff, who paid for the house on Henry Street. He and his friends were very generous people. They felt a great responsibility for others who were less fortunate, especially other Jews. They raised money so that Lillian Wald could open a public playground in the backyard of the house on Henry Street. This was practically the only green, grassy area with trees and open space where the neighborhood children could play. Soon they came to the House to take music lessons, to put on plays, and to learn to paint and draw.

As a child, Lillian had been taught that life was a garden of delights to the eye, ear, heart, and mind. Each person should have a chance to experience these joys. The Henry Street Settlement was the place where thousands of people had these opportunities for the first time in their lives.

At the heart of all Lillian's activities was her concern for health and her respect for life. Her motto was, if you see something that needs to be done, do it. Her life was very busy because there were always things which needed to be done.

In poor families, the children worked to support the home. Here an immigrant family is making artificial flowers.

The Children's Bureau

One morning, while reading the newspaper, Lillian saw an article which made her think. The government was sending an expert to Georgia to see what was happening to the cotton crop. Surely, she thought, children are as important as cotton. They are the most valuable crop this country has. Why aren't there any experts in Washington to look out for the children? Why shouldn't there be laws to protect children from working long hours at low pay in unsafe factories? It didn't take her long to form a plan for a Children's Bureau that would protect the health and welfare of children.

Lillian Wald took this plan to President Theodore Roosevelt. He thought it was a great idea, but was not able to convince Congress to set up such a program. When William Howard Taft became President, Lillian Wald tried again. This time she was successful. The Federal Children's Bureau was established and to this day it is one of the most effective means of protection for the children of the United States.

Laws to Protect Women

Even though she was most concerned with children, Lillian Wald was also aware of the needs of women. After many years of arguing with businessmen and manufacturers, she was able to get a law which made ten hours the longest a woman could work each day. Today that doesn't seem like much of an accomplishment, but in the days when women worked sixteen hours a day, and longer, ten hours was a great improvement. Lillian also urged greater limits where child labor was concerned. Other people also thought about the need for these improvements, but it took the determination of one person to fight on and on to get something done. Lillian Wald was the fighter who kept going even when others were discouraged.

Lillian Wald

Jobs for the Unemployed

When Franklin Delano Roosevelt was President, this country was having a great financial crisis. Many people were out of work. Lillian knew how terrible it was for the man in the family to lose his job. When a man did not have enough to feed his family and pay the rent, and had to accept charity, he lost his self-respect. Lillian Wald went to President Roosevelt with an idea she had used in New York many years before. People needed to work, she said, and there was always so much work that needed to be done. The people and the work should be brought together. Instead of giving welfare, pay the people to do the work. For example, the streets were always filthy. Have those who needed jobs work on cleaning up the city. Roads needed repairs. Let the people who had no jobs repair the roads. It had worked in New York. Why not elsewhere? Thanks to Lillian Wald's urgings, Public Works Projects for the poor were set up all over the country.

The superwoman of Henry Street was a nurse and a social worker. With her almost boundless energy and imagination, she was the moving force behind great projects which have made this world a better place for all of us.

PUZZLE

UNSCRAMBLE the following words and you will find five things which Lillian Wald started.

1. HICLDRNES UAERUB
2. LICPBU THLAEH NGISRUN
3. REEF YALPDNUORG
4. OLOHCS ESRUN
5. YRNEH ETERTS TNEMELTTES

There are at least 20 other words in this word for one of Lillian Wald's most outstanding traits:

COMPASSION

How many can you find?

SCORE:

    20—superperson   10—good
    15—excellent   5—try harder

QUOTATIONS

How do the following quotations relate to the story of Lillian Wald?

Discuss them with your teacher.

"As others toil for me, I must toil for others."
                            MIDRASH: *Ecclesiastes Rabbah* 2:20

"If you have no regular work find something to do—perhaps in a neglected yard or field."
                            YEHUDA BATHYRA, *Abot de Rabbi Nathan*

"Help and respect can come to a people only through self-help and self-respect."
                            STEPHEN S. WISE, *Sermons and Addresses*

"If you want to help pull a friend out of the mire, don't hesitate to get a little dirty."
                            BAAL SHEM TOV

"No labor, however humble, dishonors a person."
                            TALMUD: *Nedarim* 49b

"Children without a childhood are tragic."
                            MENDELE MOCHER SEFARIM

IDEAS OF VALUE

Think about this:

Although Lillian Wald could have lived in a big house in a wealthy neighborhood, she chose to live on the Lower East Side of New York. "If you want to help pull a friend out of the mire, don't hesitate to get a little dirty" (Baal Shem Tov). Even if she didn't know the people personally, she did not shy away from the environment in which they lived. She was a woman who wanted to be independent and useful. When she saw a cause which needed attention, she gave it hers. She learned that "No labor, however humble, dishonors a person" (Talmud: *Nedarim* 49b). When people were out of work, she felt that it was important for them to be given a chance to earn money by repairing roads and cleaning streets, if necessary, rather than be forced to accept charity. She was concerned with people and their self-respect. She worked to establish a Public Health Nursing Service for the poor. Her efforts brought about the Federal Children's Bureau to protect the rights of children. Through the Henry Street Settlement House, which she started, many people had their first experience with art and music.

A few blocks from your neighborhood there is an older section of town. The people who live there are mostly poor senior citizens. Each time you walk by you think that these elderly people could use some help. How can you help them? What are some of the things you and your friends can do to make life pleasanter for them?

Lillian Wald was a nurse and a social worker. She saw the need for institutions and laws to help the poor, the weak, and the unfortunate. Lillian Wald used her talents to establish the Public Health Nursing Service, the Federal Children's Bureau, and the Henry Street Settlement House.

List at least one institution or service that the people in your community need.

Would it be a good idea to enlist other people in your efforts to fill that need? Why?

Suppose the people in your community were trying to persuade a government official or a community leader to build it. What would you say to that person? I would say _____.

LOUIS BRANDEIS

Advocate of the People

1856–1941

Adolph and Frederika Brandeis, the parents of Louis Brandeis.

The Brandeis Family Comes to America

In 1848 there were revolts in Austria and other places in Central Europe. The people wanted freedom from persecution. The uprisings were unsuccessful and the people were still abused. Many of them decided to go to America. Among them was the family of Adolph Brandeis. One was a doctor, one was a lawyer, some were businesspeople. They wanted to become farmers. Soon they found that they could make greater contributions to their new country if they practiced the occupations for which they had been trained in Europe.

Adolph married Frederika Dembitz and they had four children. The youngest one was named Louis David. He is the one in whom we are most interested. The family moved to Louisville, Kentucky, and lived there throughout the Civil War. They were against slavery. They remembered their own need to be free and had no sympathy for anyone who wanted to keep another person as a slave.

52

Louis Decides to Be a Lawyer

When Louis Brandeis was fifteen years old he began thinking about what he wanted to do with his life. He was very interested in mathematics. His father was a grain dealer and wanted him to go into the family business. One of his uncles was a doctor. All these things sounded good. However, best of all, he liked what his uncle Lewis Dembitz did. He was a lawyer. He helped people by making sure they were treated justly and equally. Louis admired his uncle so much that he changed his middle name from David to Dembitz.

Just after the Civil War many businesses began to fail because people had no money to buy things. Adolph Brandeis closed his grain store and took his family to Europe. While they were there, Louis attended a school in Dresden, Germany. He learned a great deal, but he could never understand the strict discipline in Germany. One night especially he felt its oppressiveness. He lost the key to his rooming house. He tried to awaken a friend inside by whistling. All of a sudden he felt a hand on his shoulder. It was a policeman. Whistling at night was against the law. Fortunately, Louis was not arrested but only given a scolding. He knew then that it was time to go home. His parents agreed and the family returned to America.

Harvard Law School

Louis did not return to Louisville with them. Instead he went to Boston and persuaded Harvard Law School to admit him. He was the youngest student ever allowed to attend and probably the best. He studied so hard that his eyes began to fail. Then he hit upon the idea of getting a group of his friends together. They could take turns reading the assignments aloud. This was the beginning of a new and very successful system of studying law at Harvard.

Lawyer for the People

After graduation Louis Brandeis opened an office in Boston. This was an era of many changes in the United States. Businesses were becoming very big, and the big companies were taking over the small companies. Louis Brandeis felt this bigness was a great evil. It was causing unemployment and unrest all over the country. There were many strikes and labor disputes. Brandeis realized that the laws had to be changed to protect the people. He decided to devote his life and his law practice to protect the people against the large corporations.

In 1902 Brandeis received a call from a friend whose factory was on strike. He wanted Louis to help him settle it. He knew that any solution Brandeis offered would be worth considering. That night Louis stayed up very late to study all the details of the business.

When he arrived in New Hampshire, where the factory was, he met with the union representative and the factory owner. He listened to both sides of the story. The owner explained that the people who worked for him were well paid. The union man agreed. Then why were they striking? The people worked only during some seasons of the year. When there were orders to be filled everybody worked. As soon as the orders were completed, everybody was fired and the factory was closed. The next season, when more orders came in, the factory was opened again.

Brandeis recommended that the owner work out a schedule whereby the factory could be open all year so the work could be carried on at an even rate. That way there would be merchandise ready whenever the orders came in, and the employees would have steady work. This was a new way to settle a strike and it was successful. Everyone was pleased with the suggestions made by Louis Brandeis.

Brandeis was most interested in what we now call public interest law. Because he didn't accept fees for public interest cases, he was nicknamed "People's Advocate." He refused to accept payment because he wanted to remain independent in his opinions and not be influenced by money. It was difficult for most big companies to understand this. Louis Brandeis was often accused, unjustly, of making large sums of money from the cases he worked on.

The Boston Streetcar Case

Louis Brandeis undertook his first big public interest case in 1897. Boston's horse-drawn cars were being replaced with electric streetcars. The property on which the streetcar lines ran belonged to the city. The company which was running the cars had the right to charge whatever fare it wanted. A private company was using public property to get rich. Louis Brandeis wrote an article in which he told all the details of the crooked deal between the company and some politicians. He raised a great uproar, but the State Legislature gave the company permission to raise the fares. The legislators suspected that Brandeis was secretly representing another company. This wasn't so, but the accusation did not discourage Louis. It made him fight harder to achieve what he felt was in the interest of the people. He organized a Franchise League which helped him

Louis Brandeis

explain to the public what was wrong and dishonest about letting a private company get rich at the expense of the average citizen. The fight went on until 1902 when, at a court hearing, Brandeis proved that the company was charging high fares because it was mismanaged. Finally, the Legislature passed the bill which Brandeis wanted and the people of Boston were saved large amounts of money.

The Fight for Women's Rights

The State of Oregon had passed a law limiting the length of time a woman could work each day. Ten hours was the most. A laundry owner insisted that a certain woman should work longer or she would be fired. She went to court and the laundry owner was convicted of violating the law. The judge fined him and told the woman she didn't have to work overtime. The laundry owner became very angry and appealed the case to the Supreme Court. Louis Brandeis was asked to defend the law before the Supreme Court. He agreed because he also felt that it was important to limit the time a woman could work each day.

He wrote a long and detailed report to present to the Justices of the Supreme Court. It contained pages and pages of reasons why a woman should not be forced to work more than a limited amount of time. It explained what happened in the family and how the children were affected when the mother had to work so hard. It told how the mother's health was affected. Six weeks later the Court handed down its decision. Louis's client won and the State of Oregon kept its labor law.

The New York Garment Industry Case

The case which most influenced Brandeis's personal life was one involving the clothing industry. Here, the workers were Jewish and the bosses were Jewish. A great many immigrants in New York did piecework in the garment industry. They worked in their own homes or in crowded, poorly ventilated factories called "sweatshops." The workers got paid by the piece. The more they completed, the more they earned. Even if they worked hard, they earned very little. Finally the workers began to form a union. This made the owners very angry.

Brandeis spent weeks getting the employers to see the workers' needs. He also tried to make the workers understand the owners' problems. Finally, in September 1910, both sides agreed to a settlement and signed the "Protocol of Peace." There would be no more sweatshops and no more work in people's homes. The working hours were shortened and the wages increased. The employer could hire anyone he pleased so long as he or she belonged to the union.

This was the first time that Louis Brandeis really felt close to the Jewish people. He now became a devoted Zionist and began to use all his spare time to convince others that the Jews should have their own country in Palestine.

President Hoover congratulates Justice Brandeis.

THE WHITE HOUSE
WASHINGTON

My dear Mr. Justice:

Mrs. Hoover and I wish to be early in conveying to you our warmest congratulations on your seventy-fifth birthday. It is not necessary for us to remind you of the many satisfactions which have crowned your public service and that you reflect a heart and mind which have made the nation your debtor.

Even during your service as a member of the highest Court in the land you have found time to give service to the advancement of the Jewish homeland and I have no doubt this has brought happiness and comfort to thousands.

We wish you many happy returns of the day.

Yours faithfully,

Herbert Hoover

HERBERT HOOVER.

Supreme Court Justice

Louis Brandeis also was active in American politics. He helped get Woodrow Wilson elected President. Because of his reputation as an advocate of the people, President Wilson nominated Louis Dembitz Brandeis for the Supreme Court. It took several months for this nomination to be approved by the Senate. Brandeis was considered to be too much in favor of the "little people" as opposed to the big corporations. President Wilson was not willing to give up the fight. Finally, in 1916, Brandeis became the first Jew ever to serve on the Supreme Court of the United States.

Louis D. Brandeis saw that the "little people" of the world needed a big voice to be raised for their protection. He raised his for them.

Brandeis University, named after Louis Dembitz Brandeis.

TEST YOURSELF

Match the words in Column A with the words in Column B

A	B
Harvard	Louis D. Brandeis
Strike	Supreme Court case
People's Advocate	Zionism
Boston Streetcars	Law school
1848	First Jewish member
10-hour workday for women	Garment workers
Sweatshops	Seasonal work
Palestine	Lower fares
Supreme Court	Revolt in Austria

PUZZLE

Decode the following sentence by reversing the alphabet: Z becomes A etc.

OLFRH W. YIZMWVRH IZRHVW SRH YRT ELRXV GL KILGVXG GSV ORGGOV KVLKOV LU GSV DLIOW.

QUOTATIONS

How do the following quotations relate to the story of Louis D. Brandeis?

Discuss them with your teacher.

"If we do not help a person in trouble it is as if we caused the trouble."
NACHMAN OF BRATISLAV

"A good friend is a tower of strength: to find one is a treasure."
APOCRYPHA: Ecclesiasticus 6:14

"Good deeds bring a man immortality."
THE SASSOVER RABBI

"Just as you listen to the poor man, listen to the rich man, for it is written, 'Ye shall not favor persons in judgment.'"
ABOT DE RABBI NATHAN 20:22a

"If you see wicked men perverting justice, do not say: 'Since they are many, I must follow after them.'"
RASHI, Commentary on Exodus

"For learning the ear is more useful than the eye."
JONAH GERONDI, The Gates of Redemption

IDEAS OF VALUE

Think about this:

Louis Dembitz Brandeis studied hard and was an excellent student. He was the youngest person allowed to enter Harvard Law School at that time. When he graduated he could have worked for large corporations and earned a great deal of money. He preferred to help the "little people," the underdogs, the ones who seemed to be at a disadvantage. "A good friend is a tower of strength; to find one is a treasure" (Apocrypha: Ecclesiasticus 6:14). Brandeis became the friend of the people. He helped settle many strikes, protecting the rights of the workers as well as the owners. Women were having trouble in places where they were made to work more hours than they were able. "If we do not help a person in trouble it is as if we caused the trouble" (Nachman of Bratislav). Brandeis had a great influence in upholding the law which limited the number of hours a woman was allowed to work. He also became involved in Jewish causes after he helped settle the labor problems in the clothing industry. His greatest contribution was in the Zionist movement. Brandeis was the first Jew appointed to the United States Supreme Court.

There is a person in your class who never wins at any game. He is chubby and not very neat. The others in the class laugh whenever this person tries anything new because he is clumsy. He is a true underdog. How would you respond to your classmates when they pick on this person? Would you join them? Would you help the underdog even if that made you unpopular? Why?

Louis Dembitz Brandeis preferred to help the "little people." He helped settle strikes and labor problems in the clothing industry. He was successful at settling disputes because both sides, the workers and the owners, trusted him.

How trusting are you in regard to institutions and people? Answer the following questions.

Do drug companies always advertise their products truthfully? What makes you think that?

Do newspapers report the news exactly as it happens or as they see it? Why?

Do politicians tell you all the truth? Why do you think that?

Is big business interested in profits? Is it interested in helping people by providing goods and services at reasonable prices? Can it do both?

Do your friends always tell you the truth?

MORDECAI ANILEWITZ

Uprising

1919–1943

The Warsaw Ghetto

By the year 1939 the Jewish community in Warsaw, Poland, was about 700 years old. There were almost 400,000 Jews living in the area. Then World War II began. The German army came into the city. It built a wall around the Jewish neighborhood. All the Jews of Warsaw and Jewish refugees from other parts of Poland were forced to live in the restricted section known as the Warsaw Ghetto. There was very little food available. The Nazis took the warm coats along with all the other things of value which they could find. This made living through the cold, wet winters very difficult for the people in the Ghetto. Some Jews were able to sneak out for a short time. They tried to find a little extra food or a few pieces of coal to warm their houses. But, for the most part, just keeping alive was the most difficult thing of all.

In spite of all the hardships there were some people in the Ghetto who did heroic deeds and showed great care for

Two young Jewish underground fighters who were caught by the Nazis.

Mordecai Anilewitz

other people. They risked their lives every day so that they might protect others and prepare for a revolt against the Nazi tyrants. They knew how important each person was and how important it was for each person to do what he or she could to save as many lives as possible.

A Bold Youth

Mordecai Anilewitz was one of these people. When he was a young boy living in Warsaw, Polish teen-age gangs used to start fights with any Jewish children they met on the street. Mostly, the Jewish children ran away. But not Mordecai. He stood up to them and fought back. When he heard of anyone else being attacked, he would get his own gang together and go after the bullies. Soon, the Poles realized that they would not get away with this kind of game if Mordecai was anywhere around.

As Mordecai grew older he saw more and more clearly that the Jews of Poland would never have a really good, free life. He didn't know what to do about it, but he felt that Poland was not a good place to remain. He and many of his friends joined groups to prepare themselves to settle in Palestine. They learned farming and practiced self-defense.

While all this was going on in Poland, the Nazis were coming into power in Germany. The Jews were being persecuted and sent to concentration camps, and many of them were being put to death. After the Germans conquered Poland in World War II, many Jews from Warsaw were sent to "relocation centers." These were really death camps, but the Nazis forced them to send postcards back to Warsaw reporting that they were well and happy. This misled the other Jews into thinking that the Nazis would not harm them in the "relocation centers." The trick worked. That's why the Jews often went to the death camps without fighting back. They had been lied to and fooled into going peacefully to their deaths.

A Nazi guard and his helpless victim.

Jewish resistance fighters being executed by the Nazis.

The Ghetto Fights Back

Mordecai found out the truth, however, and he began to organize small resistance groups. Mordecai and his groups rescued Jews from the German "round-ups." Many were saved. Mordecai also operated a small radio receiver. With this he was able to get news about the war for the people in the Ghetto. Unfortunately, the news at this time was not good. Mordecai was sure that everyone in the Ghetto would die at the hands of the Nazis. He felt that if the Jews had to die they should die in battle, taking as many of their oppressors with them as they could.

When the Jews first began to fight back the deportations stopped for a few months. During this time the Jewish defense groups built bunkers and found places to hide. They collected whatever weapons they could.

On April 18, 1943, the leaders of the underground army met, with Mordecai as the chairman. It was the eve of the first Seder, and the Jews were all inside the Ghetto walls to observe the Passover holiday. The Nazis were determined to destroy the Ghetto. The defense group leaders decided to distribute all the arms and ammunition, the bottles of gasoline called "Molotov cocktails," and whatever food they had. They also gave out poison capsules, so that anyone who was caught would have a way to escape being tortured by the Nazis.

The next day the Germans attacked. They came so heavily equipped that they might have been fighting the army of a big country instead of the Jews of the Warsaw Ghetto. They were convinced that they could not be stopped by a few Jews. They got the surprise of their lives. Their tanks were stopped by home-made bombs. The soldiers were hit by carefully aimed shots from inside the barricaded buildings. The Germans ran away in panic. They reported to their superiors that the Jewish resistance was strong and unexpected.

A Jewish defense fighter in Warsaw jumps to his death rather than surrender to the Nazis.

After the battle, the Nazis rounded up the survivors of the uprising.

The End of the Battle

A letter was later found which Mordecai wrote to a friend on April 23, 1943, less than a week after the uprising began. In it he wrote that the main dream of his life had come true. He had been fortunate enough to see Jews rise up to defend themselves.

After the battle began things didn't get any better. Before long the food and ammunition were almost gone and the people were weakened by illness and starvation. On May 8, the Germans broke through and captured the main bunker. They threw in poison gas and shot everyone who came out. Mordecai Anilewitz died that day along with a great many others. A few managed to escape through the sewers and joined with others in the forests to continue the fight.

Kibbutz Yad Mordecai

Those who lived reported the great heroism of the fighters in the Warsaw Ghetto. They told of the tremendous contribution made by one man who had devoted his life to helping the Jews live bravely and with a purpose. That man was Mordecai Anilewitz. Yad Mordecai, a kibbutz in Israel, was built in his memory. At the gateway of the kibbutz stands a statue of a tall, brave-looking young man with a Molotov cocktail in his hand, a young man who showed the world what it means to "die with honor." Mordecai saw the need for people to stand up and defend themselves, and he helped them do it.

Statue of Mordecai Anilewitz at the entrance of Kibbutz Yad Mordecai.

PUZZLE

This puzzle can be solved by adding and subtracting the letters of the objects shown here. Spell each word and then cross out those letters which are shown with a minus sign in front of them. Place each remaining letter in a square after the equal sign in the same order as they appear in the picture.

As a hint you will find that the word is one which describes Mordecai Anilewitz.

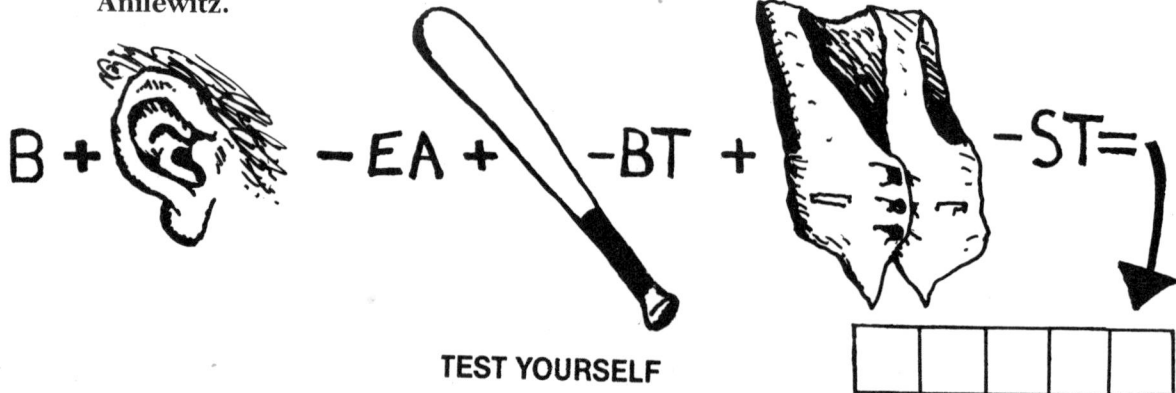

TEST YOURSELF

Underline the answer which best completes the following sentences:

1. The Nazis made life (a) good, (b) terrible, (c) fair for the Jews in Poland.

2. Jews lived in the Warsaw Ghetto because (a) they wanted to, (b) they had lived there all their lives and didn't want to move, (c) they were forced to by the Germans.

3. Mordecai Anilewitz became a hero in the Ghetto because (a) he knew where to find food, (b) he made friends with the Nazis, (c) he organized the uprising against the Germans.

4. The dream of Mordecai's life was (a) to get rich, (b) to see the Jews defend themselves, (c) to make friends with the Germans.

5. Yad Mordecai is (a) a kibbutz in Israel named in memory of Mordecai Anilewitz, (b) a street in Britain, (c) the name of a new Israeli soda.

6. One of the most famous events toward the end of World War II was (a) Hitler's birthday, (b) the Battle of the Warsaw Ghetto, (c) the freeing of the Jews by the Germans.

QUOTATIONS

How do the following quotations relate to the story of Mordecai Anilewitz and the Warsaw Ghetto?

Discuss them with your teacher.

"As long as there is life there is hope."
　　　　　　　　　　　　　　　　TALMUD: Berakot 9:1

"It is better to die on your feet than to live on your knees."
　　　　　　　　　　　　　　　　OLD YIDDISH PROVERB

"Be strong and of good courage."
　　　　　　　　　　　　　　　　BIBLE: Joshua 1:9

"Courage is fire and bullying is smoke."
　　　　　　　　　　　　　　　　BENJAMIN DISRAELI

"The refugee is like a plant without soil or water."
　　　　　　　　　　　　　　　　MOSES IBN EZRA, Shirat Yisrael

IDEAS OF VALUE

Think about this:

"Be strong and of good courage" (Bible: Joshua 1:9) was a guiding rule by which Mordecai Anilewitz lived. He protected the younger children from Polish teenage gangs which attacked them. In the Warsaw Ghetto he organized small groups of Jews to resist the Germans and cause disturbances when they came. That way many were not taken away to concentration camps as early as they might have been. He also felt that "As long as there is life, there is hope" (Talmud: *Berakot* 9:1). He organized fighting groups to resist the Germans when they decided to destroy the Ghetto. His leadership gave the Jews the courage to rise up and fight against the injustices of their oppressors.

There are a few children in the playground who always seem to want what you have. If you are playing ping-pong, they want to use the table. If you are playing basketball, they want the court. They try to chase you away. What should you do—give them what they want or refuse to give in and risk a fight? When would you stay, and when would you go? When is it important to fight?

Mordecai Anilewitz was the leader of the Warsaw Ghetto revolt. He risked his life to protect his fellow Jews and to organize the revolt against the Nazis. All his life he was a leader and a fighter.

Can you think of a situation in which you were a leader?

Describe your actions.

Name two leaders that you admire.

I admire _____ because:

I admire _____ because:

HENRIETTA SZOLD

Helpful Henrietta

1860–1945

A Girl Who Thought for Herself

The woman who has been called the "Mother of Israel" was never married, but she had about 50,000 children. How it happened is a long story. She was born in December 1860, and grew up in the city of Baltimore, Maryland. She was the oldest of five daughters born to Sophia and Benjamin Szold. Her name was Henrietta.

Although Benjamin was a rabbi he believed that girls should be educated as well as boys. He saw to it that Henrietta had a good background in Hebrew and German. She also went to high school.

Her first job after graduation was as a teacher in a girls' school. The other teachers were interested in making "little ladies" of the students, but Henrietta wanted to make them think for themselves. This was a new idea. Henrietta had to convince the principal that she was not trying to prepare the girls to compete with men. She wanted to teach them how to read the newspaper and understand what was going on in the world. Finally, she was given permission. It was a giant step forward.

Henrietta Szold as a young woman.

Helping the Russian Immigrants

In 1882 the Russian May Laws were passed. These laws made life for the Jews in Russia very hard. There were pogroms in the small Jewish communities. The people had to pay extra-heavy taxes and there was little food. The Jews had almost no way to earn a living. Many of them came to the United States. Some settled in Baltimore. The Russians couldn't speak English and were very poor. The Jews of Baltimore were not very pleased to have the immigrants move to their city. This attitude disturbed Henrietta very much. She urged the ladies in her Literary Club to be friendly and helpful, but she had little success.

Every night the Russians came to Rabbi Szold for one thing or another. He did what he could to help them. They spoke only Russian and Yiddish, so it was difficult for them to get jobs and find places to live. Henrietta watched this parade of people. She decided that what they needed first was to learn the language of their new country. But how does one teach older people? And when and where? Then she hit upon an idea. Why not at night? After other needs were taken care of, the immigrants, young and old, could come to classes and learn how to read, write, and speak English. This would prepare them to become citizens of their new country.

At first Henrietta's friends laughed at the suggestion. Who ever went to school at night? Her parents thought it was a great idea. Finally, she was able to get some of her friends to help. With her usual determination she rented a room and invited the Russians to come. She raised money for books and blackboards. Soon she had a night school going. Fathers and young sons studied in the same class. As the project became better known, more and more people flocked to the classes, and soon Henrietta had to expand the school to several rooms. The night school was such a success that it was copied in other cities.

A Woman at JTS

In the meantime Henrietta's sisters and friends were getting married. She realized that time was passing and she felt as if she were not accomplishing enough. She decided to resign from the school where she had taught for so many years. She resigned from the night school too. By this time the city had taken it over and there was enough money for teachers and books.

In 1893 Henrietta Szold got a job as editor and translator for the Jewish Publication Society in Philadelphia. Here she prepared manuscripts for printing. Some she had to translate from Hebrew or German into English. During this time her father became quite ill. In 1902 he died. Henrietta suffered a great loss, as did the rest of her family. Her father had been a great scholar. She decided that his papers and sermons should be prepared for publication so that others might share them. In order to do this she needed some special education. She applied to the Jewish Theological Seminary, a school for Conservative rabbis. At

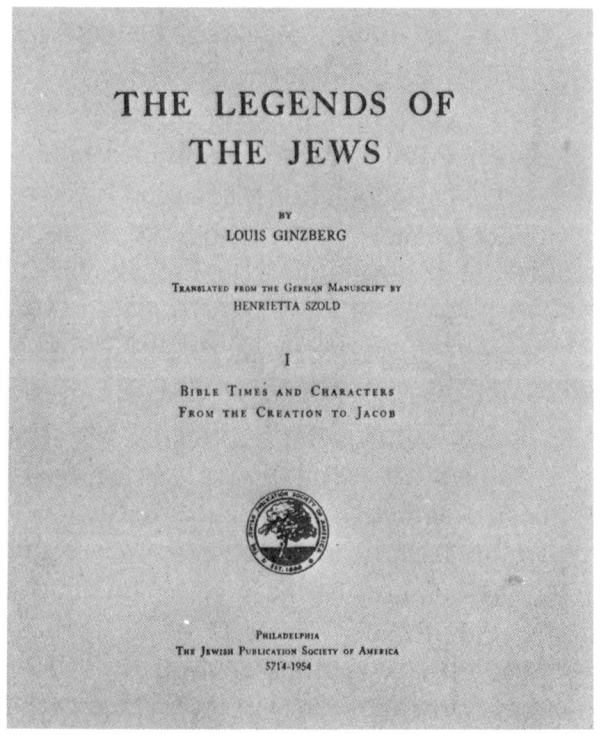

Title page of "The Legends of the Jews" translated by Henrietta Szold.

Henrietta Szold digging the first shovelful of earth for a health center in Israel.

first her application met with considerable resistance. After due consideration she was admitted as the first woman ever to attend. The students and the teachers were very nice to her and she made many friends. Among them was one whom she grew to love. Unfortunately, the young man married someone else.

A Visit to Palestine

Henrietta worked long hours, sometimes as many as sixteen or eighteen each day. After a while she became ill from this exhausting routine and had to take a rest. She decided to go on a trip with her mother. They visited many relatives in Poland and Austria. Then they went on to Palestine. This had always been a dream of Henrietta's. She wanted to visit the ancient homeland of her people.

As she went from place to place in Palestine, Henrietta saw that many children were suffering from a terrible eye disease. Many became blind. To her pleasant surprise she found one school where none of the students had this eye problem. The director told her, when she asked, that a doctor came to the school every day and examined the children. As soon as any symptoms appeared the children were treated and cured. On hearing this, Henrietta's mother suggested that the women in the Literary Club should try to help the children in Palestine. When Henrietta got home, she and her friends began to do something to change the poor health conditions in Eretz Yisrael, the land of Israel.

Hadassah Is Born

A few years later Henrietta started the organization which was to be known as Hadassah. The women who joined took it as their responsibility to raise money to improve the health conditions of Jews and Arabs in Palestine. Branches of this organization grew up all over the United States.

One of the first steps taken by the group was to send two public health nurses to Palestine. There, with the help of Mrs. Nathan Straus, they bought a house which they turned into a clinic and hospital for the poor. This was only the beginning of the health service program that Hadassah developed in Palestine through the efforts of Henrietta Szold. The organization grew. It became a source of comfort and help for the developing country and its health needs, even until today.

Henrietta Settles in Palestine

After World War I, at the age of sixty, Henrietta Szold moved to Palestine so that she could be on the scene to offer her help. She discovered that when teenagers got into trouble, they were sent to a prison with adult criminals, Arabs and Jews alike. They couldn't communicate with the officials or the other prisoners because of the language differences. The

A letter from Henrietta Szold in which she writes that "Palestine is truly the gathering place of the exiles."

probation officers who tried to help didn't know Hebrew. The young prisoners didn't know Arabic. It was like the tower of Babel. Henrietta realized that each time an offender went to court it was necessary for a social worker from the Jewish community to be there. This was the way to insure a more just hearing and to protect the rights of the Jews.

As Henrietta traveled around the poor neighborhoods she saw how important it was for the children to learn how to earn a living. They needed to be taught a trade or skill. She called upon her supporters in Hadassah to undertake still another project. They agreed to raise the money. A Vocational Training School for Girls was established in Jerusalem. Because of the success of this school, many others were established for boys and girls by other organizations.

In the vocational schools the children were taught better eating habits. It was the job of the Hadassah dietitian to convince people that cereal and milk made a better breakfast than herring. They also introduced school lunches into the Arab schools. All the children, Jews and Arabs, benefitted from the new ideas that Henrietta Szold and her friends from Hadassah brought to the country.

Youth Aliyah Rescues the Children

While this was going on in Palestine, more and more restrictions were being placed upon the Jews of Germany. Henrietta went to Europe on some business. There she discovered that many people were aware that things would get worse as time went on. Parents asked if she could arrange for their children to go to Eretz Yisrael. It was a challenge which she could not pass up. She returned to Jerusalem and made plans to settle the young German Jews in the most suitable places she could find. Of course, all this required money. Again, she turned to her American friends in Hadassah to support a program which she called Youth Aliyah. Once again, they agreed to provide the money for Henrietta's dream.

The first group of Youth Aliyah children, 45 in all, arrived with neatly

Henrietta Szold with "her children."

packed suitcases. They had all the clothes they would need. They were well fed and healthy looking, like children going to camp. As was to become her pattern in the next few years, Henrietta met them at the dock. She stayed with them for a few days until they were settled in their new homes.

By the end of World War II more than 50,000 children had been rescued from the European holocaust as a result of Henrietta Szold's program to save the children. Those who came later were in much poorer health than the early arrivals. As things got worse in Europe, the condition of the children also got worse. When they arrived in Eretz Yisrael they were taken in by families who shared their homes and their love with these children. Special Youth Aliyah villages were formed to house some of these refugees.

In 1945, at the age of 85, Henrietta Szold died. At her funeral a fifteen-year-old orphan boy stood at her graveside and recited Kaddish. She had no children of her own, but the 50,000 Youth Aliyah children called her Mama. He was one of them.

These are some of the things Henrietta Szold saw the need for. Even though she was only one person, she used her influence to help get them done.

Henrietta Szold

The Hadassah Hospital in Jerusalem, a living memorial to Henrietta Szold.

PUZZLE

From the words below select seven which will fit correctly to form the word which describes Henrietta Szold. Choose the words and write the missing letters in the blank spaces.

Henrietta was always

```
        H _ _ _ _ _ _ _ _
      _ E _ _ _ _ _ _ _
  _ _ _ _ _ L
    _ _ _ P _ _ _ _ _
      _ _ F _ _ _
      _ _ U _ _
      _ L _ _ _ _
```

HOTEL	REFUGEES	HOSPITAL
ALIYAH	REFORM	SCHOOL
EUROPE	YOUTH	HADASSAH

TEST YOURSELF

Complete the following sentences with words chosen from the list below:

1. Jews left Russia in 1882 because of the _____.
2. Henrietta Szold started the first _____ to teach new immigrants.
3. She tried to make her students _____ for themselves.
4. In Palestine she found that _____ was very badly needed.
5. She organized _____, a women's organization to help the children in Palestine.
6. Henrietta Szold saw the need for girls to learn a _____ so that they could earn money to support themselves.
7. Henrietta was the first woman to attend the _____.
8. She saved the lives of more than 50,000 children during World War II through the _____ program.
9. Henrietta Szold edited and translated books for the _____ _____ in Philadelphia.
10. She helped _____ the juvenile prison system in Palestine.

THINK	CHANGE
JEWISH THEOLOGICAL SEMINARY	JEWISH PUBLICATION SOCIETY
YOUTH ALIYAH	NIGHT SCHOOL
MAY LAWS	HADASSAH
HEALTH CARE	TRADE

QUOTATIONS

How do the following quotations relate to the story of Henrietta Szold?

Discuss them with your teacher.

"We live largely for the good and happiness of others."
    JUDAH ARYEH MOSCATO, *Nefutzot Yehuda*

"The aim of education must be the training of independently acting and thinking individuals."
    ALBERT EINSTEIN, *Out of My Later Years*

"As one hand washes the other so must one person help another."
    LEON OF MODENA, *Tzemah Tzaddik*

"Study must precede practice."
    TALMUD: Pesachim 3:7

"The greatest charity is to enable the poor to earn a living."
    TALMUD: Shabbat 63a

IDEAS OF VALUE

Think about this:

Henrietta Szold was an organizer. "We live largely for the good and happiness of others" (Moscato, *Nefutzot Yehuda*). She was also a concerned person. She saw that Russian immigrants needed to learn how to read and write. She organized a night school for them. In Palestine, she saw Arab and Jewish children who needed better health care. She organized Hadassah to provide the money for medicine, doctors, and nurses. She saw children in Europe who needed to get away from Nazi persecution. She organized Youth Aliyah and brought as many as she could to Palestine. Henrietta Szold was motivated to do all these things because when she was a young girl her father saw to it that she had a good education. She was taught "to love the stranger, for we were strangers in Egypt" (Bible: Deuteronomy 10:19). She showed her concern even for people she didn't know. Whether they were Jews or Arabs didn't matter. Foreigners were as important as her childhood neighbors. What was most important was that all people be given the opportunity to be healthy and to be able to earn a decent living.

Russian Jews are emigrating from the Soviet Union. They have many of the same problems which the Russian Jews of the early twentieth century had. Jews from Iran are also coming to this country in great numbers. They move into your neighborhood. They need help. What can you do to help them?

Henrietta Szold never had a family of her own. Yet she was the "mother" of thousands of children. She communicated her love and concern to her "family," and they in turn communicated their love and respect to her.

Happy families have good lines of communication. Grandparents, parents, children, and relatives communicate with each other in good times and in bad. They help each other in times of trouble and sadness. They celebrate and enjoy togetherness in times of happiness.

Name three ideas which lead to good communications within families.

Name three roadblocks to good communications within families.

Why is communication important to a happy and healthy family life?

LOUISE WATERMAN WISE

The Story of Louise

1875–1947

A Woman Who Cared

Can you imagine a woman who would turn down the King of England when he offered to give her the Order of the British Empire? This woman was Louise Waterman Wise. She was the wife of Rabbi Stephen S. Wise. Why she was offered this honor and why she refused to accept it is an interesting story.

Like her husband, Louise Wise was concerned with justice and independence for all people. He helped get laws passed in Oregon to limit child labor and the number of hours a woman could work each day. Louise encouraged him in that. He was offered a congregation in New York City. She agreed with him when he refused to accept it because the pulpit was not free. He would have to get approval from the temple board for each sermon he delivered. They both wanted to go to New York. They both agreed, however, that a pulpit was not worth having if the rabbi could not speak out on the important issues of the day.

In 1907 the Wises moved to New York with their two children. There, Rabbi Wise started the Free Synagogue. It was because of her children that Louise made her first public appearance as a speaker. Many times the children came home from school sick. She decided to investigate. She found their classrooms to be overcrowded and extremely overheated. When she complained to the teacher and

Louise Waterman Wise

the principal, no one seemed to care, so Louise began a campaign to interest educators and public health experts in her cause. She collected enough material to back up her claims that children became ill if there wasn't enough fresh air in the classrooms. Then she went to the Board of Education and made her first speech. She was so convincing that the Association of Heating and Ventilating Engineers promised to investigate further. Eventually there was a great improvement in the classrooms and fewer children became ill.

A Woman Who Helped

A few years later, at a dinner party, a friend told Louise Wise about how lonely she and her husband were. They were not able to have children but they wanted very much to have a family. Louise suggested that they adopt a baby. Her friend said that they would be happy to but didn't know how. Louise decided to visit an orphan asylum. She thought the authorities would be happy to have a child given a good home with a loving family. Much to her amazement, she found that the director was not anxious to give up any of the children because the city was paying the institution a certain amount of money to take care of each child. The head of the asylum didn't refuse her request but made it clear that she should not ask again. Louise found a baby for her friends and they were very grateful.

She didn't stop there. She decided that it was much healthier for children to be in homes with families who wanted them than in institutions where they were cared for but not really loved. She called a few of her friends together to form a committee which would arrange for the adoption of Jewish children.

Louise and her Child Adoption Committee, which was part of the Free Synagogue's Social Service program, placed infants with parents who wanted babies. They matched light-haired babies with light-haired parents. They placed darker-haired babies with darker-haired parents. They investigated those who wanted babies to make sure that they would provide good, loving homes for the children. This agency is still at work finding homes for children and children for would-be parents.

During this time Louise always found time to help young artists. She was equally interested in writers. When she found one who was worthy of having more people read his or her works, she translated them into English from German or French.

Louise Founds the Women's Division

In the early 1930s Rabbi Wise was busy trying to make people understand the threat posed to the Jews of Europe by Hitler and the Nazis. The rabbi was very active in the American Jewish Congress. Louise realized that women could help the AJC carry out its mission of defending Jews from anti-Semites at home and aiding Jews in Europe and Palestine. She formed an organization for this purpose, the Women's Division of the American Jewish Congress.

Louise convinced the Congress Women that a boycott of German-made items was important. She went to stores and asked them not to sell things made in Germany because of the Nazi government's inhumane treatment of other people. Some agreed; others, however, refused to stop selling German-made products. Louise and her group began to picket these stores.

An anti-Nazi demonstration organized by Louise W. Wise.

In 1933, when refugees from Germany began to come to the United States, Louise Wise found that there was no place for them to stay until they were able to find relatives or friends who could help them get settled. With the aid of the Women's Division, she took over one of the houses where the Free Synagogue would someday build its sanctuary. She borrowed and begged whatever furniture she needed. She got blankets and sheets from department stores. Somewhere she found dishes and tables and chairs. All this was made available to the refugees at no cost. It was called Congress House, and thousands of people spent their first nights in the safety of the United States there. They were treated as guests and never made to feel that they were being given charity. All this was part of Louise's appreciation for the dignity of each human being.

In 1940, when it became impossible for any more refugees to leave Europe, Louise came up with another plan. She changed the name to Defense House and made it available to thousands of servicemen and women. They were going overseas or on furlough in New York. Hotel rooms were hard to find and very costly. The Women's Division of the AJC made rooms available to American soldiers and sailors, and to those from Britain as well. A delicious breakfast was served in the morning, and the men and women who came were made to feel at home.

Refugees from Germany being welcomed to America.

When Britain was under heavy German attack, Louise raised funds so that the children could be sent from London to safer places. Through her efforts, places of refuge for British children were set up and kept supplied throughout the war.

Louise Wise and the King of England

Louise and Stephen Wise were Zionists from the beginning. They felt that Palestine should be open to any Jew who wished to settle there. The League of Nations, after World War I, had given Britain a Mandate to help create a Jewish homeland in Palestine. As World War II progressed, the British began to side with the Arabs. They made it more and more difficult for Jews from Europe to get into the country. Rabbi Wise appealed to them to open the doors again. It didn't help. Jews all over the free world began to protest. This also had no effect. The British put the refugees from Europe's concentration camps into camps in Cyprus. They would not allow these poor, mistreated men, women, and children to find new homes in the land which had been promised to them.

At this time a list of people to be honored by the King of England was being drawn up. Because she had been so helpful in finding safe places for the children of London during the German air raids, and because of the hospitality she had arranged for British servicemen and women during their visits to New York, the name of Louise Waterman Wise was placed on the list.

When she was told about the honor, Louise sat down and wrote a letter. In this letter she said she could not accept the honor because she was very displeased by the British government's policy against the Jews who wished to live in Palestine. Her act gave new courage to her people.

Louise Waterman Wise lived long enough to see Israel established as a free Jewish nation. Her life was lived with dignity and courage. She saw things which needed to be done, and she did them.

PUZZLE

Find the words which are capitalized in the statements below. They are scattered throughout the square. When you locate each of these words draw a line around it. Sometimes the words start at the top, sometimes they are written from side to side (either right to left or left to right), sometimes they start at the bottom and go up and some are written diagonally.

Louise lived her life with DIGNITY and COURAGE.

She started an ADOPTION AGENCY.

She arranged a place for REFUGEES to stay.

Later, the CONGRESS House offered HOSPITALITY to servicemen and women. It was then called DEFENSE HOUSE.

Great Britain had a MANDATE to make Palestine (Israel) a homeland for Jews.

People who believe that the Jews should have a homeland in Palestine (Israel) are called ZIONISTS.

Louise picketed in front of a store because she wanted to BOYCOTT German-made things which it sold.

```
X A B J U O P K F H B L A R
C D R G K N M A L G O U K C
H O S P I T A L I T Y H W Z
K P U A T U N D X M C L Z M
Z T D R L B D F R Y O O S P
Q I Y D A J A E E R T J A K
K O O L D G T J F D T J H S
R N S N K R E N U E D L H S
N A W I I F L F G H N I E E
P G E U T S H E E K H S H R
Q E U R C M T D E H U L E G
F N K E U F J S S O M S K N
L C A D S F D J H K U Y T O
X Y T I N G I D D K O T N C
```

Louise and Stephen Wise were both very devoted to the cause of establishing a HOMELAND for the Jewish people in the land of Israel.

How many words can you find in HOMELAND? There are at least thirty. Can you find twenty?

        25—supersleuth   10—fair
        20—excellent   5—try harder
        15—pretty good

QUOTATIONS

How do the following quotations relate to the story of Louise Waterman Wise?

Discuss them with your teacher.

"When trouble comes into the world, Israel feels it first; when good comes, Israel feels it first, too."
MIDRASH: Lamentations Rabbah 2:3

"...The refugee is like a plant without soil or water."
MOSES IBN EZRA, Shirat Yisrael

"Progress is the fruit of devotion."
MOSES IBN EZRA, Shirat Yisrael

"Strength and dignity are her clothing."
BIBLE: Proverbs 31:25

"Four virtues refresh the world: charity, justice, truth, and peace."
SEDER ELIYAHU RABBAH

IDEAS OF VALUE

Think about this:

Louise Waterman Wise was like a biblical prophet. It was not that she could tell what was going to happen in the future. That was not the role of the prophet. It was his or her job to speak out against injustice and wrongdoing. The Prophet Isaiah (1:17) said: "Seek justice, relieve the oppressed, judge the fatherless, and plead for the widow." Louise Wise also spoke out when she felt that something was not right. However, she knew that words were not enough. She acted to correct these evils. When she felt that her children's classrooms were not ventilated properly, she did something about it. In the years before World War II, she started the boycott of German-made products to call to the attention of the community what she felt was wrong. "One who adopts an orphan is as if he begot him" (Talmud: *Megillah* 13a). She started an adoption agency to help children and would-be parents. She objected to the British policy of keeping Jews out of Palestine so she refused to accept an honor from the King of England. She helped the oppressed refugees by opening Congress House and offering them a place to stay. She was a woman of great compassion. Her feelings reached out to the homeless and the lonely.

If you were offered a prize by an organization which stood for things you are against, would you accept? What ideas or principles would help you to decide? Do you think you might influence the organization to change its policy by refusing? Do you think you could influence it to change by accepting but telling why you don't agree?

Louise Waterman Wise spoke out and fought injustice. You too have witnessed and read about issues which are unjust.
Write a letter to a legislator or an elective official about an injustice that is important to you, your family, your temple, or your community.

Dear, Name of person
Address

Sincerely,
Your signature

CHAIM WEIZMANN

The Chemist

1874–1952

A Vote at the United Nations

He was old, tired, and partially blind. He had come to the United States to plead the cause of the Jewish people before the United Nations. It was November 1947. He did all he could to convince the countries of the world that his people needed and deserved a homeland in Palestine. When the vote was taken, Chaim Weizmann was too exhausted to attend the meeting. Instead he listened on a radio. Each country was called by name. Each country voted according to its special interests. At last, the roll call was over. The United Nations voted 33 to 13 for the partition of Palestine. There was to be a Jewish and an Arab state. At last the Jews would have a homeland. Chaim Weizmann and his devoted wife, Vera, cried with joy. Now he could go on with his work as a chemist. She could go on with her work as a doctor. The Jewish people could go on as free citizens in a country of their own.

The Jewish State Is Born

On their way to Palestine, the Weizmanns went to London to visit their son. While there Chaim began to get distressing reports. Britain was against the partition plan. Its representatives at the United Nations were trying to make the other countries change their opinions. Dr. Weizmann was ill, but he got out of bed, packed his bags, and left for Washington. He went to see President Truman. Weizmann told him that the only choice the Jewish people had was extermination or a homeland. President Truman was very sympathetic. He told Dr.

Chaim Weizmann, first President of Israel, addressing the first Knesset of Israel.

Chaim Weizmann presents a Torah Scroll to President Harry Truman.

Weizmann that he would do all he could to make the partition work. Truman kept his word. He helped defeat those in the United Nations who wanted another vote. The United States used its influence and the original decision stood.

While Weizmann was working at the United Nations, David Ben-Gurion and the other leaders in Palestine were busy too. They were getting ready to set up a government the minute the British left. They were training an army and an air force in case they had to defend themselves. Eight hours before the British Mandate ended, a Jewish state was announced in Tel Aviv. It was to be called the State of Israel. President Harry Truman was the first official of any government to recognize the Jewish state.

Chaim Weizmann was still in New York when he learned he had been elected the first President of the new Jewish state. Chaim and Vera were very pleased. This assignment came after a lifetime of devotion and determination that a Jewish homeland was necessary.

Chaim Weizmann's Early Life

Chaim Weizmann was born in Russia in 1874. His family lived in a town in the area to which Jews were restricted. As a very small child Chaim was an excellent student. He taught himself how to read and write Yiddish and Hebrew before he was old enough to go to school. When he began school, he was placed in a class with much older boys.

Chaim was particularly influenced by one teacher who taught the boys more than Talmud and Bible. He made them aware of science, especially chemistry. When Chaim was ten years old he was

Chaim Weizmann as a young man.

given special permission to go to a Russian school in Pinsk. It was very rare for a Jewish boy to go to a Russian school, but Chaim showed such great ability that an exception was made for him. However, he soon began to feel that the other students didn't like Jews. He studied hard. He also became interested in Zionism, the movement working to establish a Jewish homeland.

In 1892 Chaim left Russia to study in a university in Germany. While there he heard about a new book called *The Jewish State* by Theodor Herzl. It stressed the idea that the Jews were not welcome anywhere in Europe. To continue as a people, they had to have their own country. Thousands of years of tradition made Palestine the only place for this new state. Herzl's book left a lifelong impression on Chaim Weizmann.

Meanwhile, Chaim became a chemist. He lived and worked in Switzerland, where he experimented with dyes and other products. He began to work on acetone, a substance used in making explosives.

In 1904 Chaim moved to England. He was thirty years old. He had no money, no job, and no home. He couldn't speak English. He left Vera behind to complete her studies in medical school.

The Balfour Declaration

In 1914 World War I began. Winston Churchill sent for Chaim Weizmann. He had heard about his experiments with acetone. Britain needed explosives for the war. Churchill was in charge of military supplies. He asked the chemist to produce 30,000 gallons of acetone. Weizmann was shocked. He was only able to produce tiny amounts in test tubes. He would

Vera and Chaim Weizmann, 1906.

need special equipment and lots of assistants. Churchill assured him he could have whatever he needed. Weizmann was determined to make the product that Britain needed. He was just as determined to explain to the British that the Jewish people needed a homeland.

Among the people Chaim Weizmann met was Sir Arthur Balfour, a member of the British Parliament. In appreciation for Chaim's help during the war, Balfour urged the British government to issue a declaration saying that it favored the establishment of a Jewish homeland in Palestine. After the war the League of Nations gave Britain the Mandate over Palestine. The Jews were allowed to settle in the country and build a homeland there.

Chaim Weizmann's Contributions to Israel

When Chaim Weizmann went to Palestine, in July 1918, he decided that the future Jewish state must have an excellent educational system. The school he started, known to this day as the Hebrew University, opened in April 1925.

In spite of the Balfour Declaration all did not go well in Palestine. Winston Churchill was afraid the Arabs might object to the Jewish homeland. He decided to limit its size. This meant limiting the number of Jews who could come there to settle.

At this time Hitler came to power in Germany. The Jews of Germany were persecuted. Their property and businesses were taken away. Many were sent to concentration camps. Chaim Weizmann became chairman of the Central Bureau for the Resettlement of German Jews, a group which tried to help German Jews escape from the Nazis. The British issued a White Paper restricting the number of Jews who could come to Palestine. As a result, many died in Europe.

Chaim Weizmann continued to work in his laboratory all the time that he was trying to help the European Jews to escape. One of the things that he worked on was synthetic rubber. During World War II the Allies were having trouble getting enough real rubber for all their military needs. In 1942 Dr. Weizmann came to the United States to help with the problem. He developed a formula to produce artificial rubber and turned it over to an American company.

Vera and Chaim then went home to Rehovoth, Israel, where they mourned for their son, who was killed while serving in the British army. In 1946, Chaim Weizmann laid the cornerstone for a scientific institute. It was built next-door

Weizmann and Emir Feisal, 1918.

Weizmann inspecting Jewish volunteers during World War II.

The Weizmann Institute

to his home in Rehovoth and is called the Weizmann Institute. There, some of the greatest scientific developments in the world were to take place in the years that followed.

Israel's First President

Because of his dedication to his people, his labors in behalf of the Jewish homeland, his contributions to the scientific discoveries which helped the Allies win two great wars, and his foresight in establishing two schools of higher learning in the Jewish state, Chaim Weizmann was chosen to be the first President of the State of Israel. His great vision of the future led him to convince others that the Jewish people were entitled to a homeland. In a difficult period for all humanity, Chaim Weizmann worked to make this world a better place.

Weizmann's inauguration as the first President of Israel, Feb. 7, 1949.

TEST YOURSELF

Fill in the word or phrase which applies to the following:

1. Britain's decision to limit the number of Jews permitted into Palestine was _____.
2. President of the United States who was the first government leader to recognize the new state of Israel. _____.
3. Weizmann's formula to help the Allies in World War II produce _____.
4. The book called *The Jewish State* was written by _____.
5. The first school of higher learning established by Weizmann was the _____.
6. The document issued by the British government saying that it looked with favor upon the establishment of a Jewish homeland in Palestine was the _____.
7. Dr. Weizmann helped the Allies win World War I by making _____.
8. The second school Dr. Weizmann founded in Israel was the ____.
9. The movement to establish a Jewish homeland is called _____.

Each of these words or phrases applies to one of the above:

White Paper
Synthetic rubber
Zionism
Theodor Herzl
Institute of Science
Harry Truman
Acetone
Hebrew University
Balfour Declaration

PUZZLE

To solve this puzzle you must write the words listed in their right places. One word is given to you as a start.

2 letters	6 letters
UN	TRUMAN
	ISRAEL
5 letters	RUSSIA
CHAIM	
	8 letters
7 letters	HOMELAND
CHEMIST	
BRITAIN	
BALFOUR	

IDEAS OF VALUE

Think about this:

Maimonides said: "If I do not acquire ideals in my youth, when will I?" Chaim Weizmann had ideals, acquired in his youth. The two leading dreams of his life were to see a home for the Jewish people in Palestine and to use his great talents in chemistry to help mankind. With his development of acetone and his formula for synthetic rubber he was able to influence the establishment of the State of Israel. Because of his help in winning the war, the British government issued the Balfour Declaration. However, the British did not learn the lesson from the Bible (Numbers 30:3), "When a man [or a nation] vows a vow . . . he shall not break his word." The British issued regulations limiting the number of Jews who could enter the land. They didn't want to anger the Arabs, who said they were helping the Jews too much.

Your best friend promises to help you win the election as class president. Some of the other candidates begin to complain to your friend about the help he is giving you. As the election comes closer you discover that your friend is also helping your opponent. You are elected anyway. How would you treat this friend? How would you treat your former opponent? Why?

QUOTATIONS

How do the following quotations relate to the story of Chaim Weizmann?

Discuss them with your teacher.

"The real guardians of the state are the teachers."
TALMUD: Hagigah

"Some men long more for their homeland than for their food."
MOSES IBN EZRA, Shirat Yisrael

"Jerusalem was destroyed because its children did not attend school."
TALMUD: Shabbat 119b

"In every country, even unto the giving of your life, be men of your country; and at the same time be Jews."
EDMUND FLEG, Why I Am a Jew

"The Jews have but one way of saving themselves—a return to their own people and an emigration to their own land."
THEODOR HERZL, The Jewish State

"Zionism aims to create for the Jewish people a publicly recognized and legally secured home in Palestine."
BASLE PROGRAM

Chaim Weizmann was a brilliant chemist. He could have stayed in his laboratory and made lots of money. But he made a decision. Money was not everything in his life. He decided to work for the establishment of the State of Israel.

You will be called upon to make important decisions in your life—to go to a particular school, to major in a particular subject, to join a club, to learn a profession. How will you go about making your decision? Pick any of the two preceding decisions and tell how you would decide and why.

My decision

The choices I had

I made the decision because

My decision

The choices I had

I made the decision because

EDDIE CANTOR

For Everybody's Benefit

1892-1964

A Summer Camp for City Boys

The boys at camp loved to sit around the fire and listen to him sing and tell jokes. They enjoyed his imitations and impersonations of their favorite stars. He was a skinny, funny-looking boy with big pop-eyes. His name was Eddie Cantor. He and all the other boys came to the camp from the dirty, hot streets of New York City. They were all from very poor families, but they were able to go to camp because there were other people in the city who cared. A Jewish charity raised money for this special purpose. Eddie loved Surprise Lake Camp. He went back for several summers. Looking forward to camp helped him get through the cold, hungry months of winter.

Eddie was an orphan from the time he was two years old. His grandmother took care of him as best she could, but life was very difficult. Eddie could easily have become a delinquent, but somehow he always found a way to get by. The camp probably was the greatest single influence in his life. In 1902, when he was ten years old, he and twenty-nine other boys formed a club to give other kids from the city a chance to go to camp. When they grew to manhood, Eddie and his friends kept their promise.

Eddie Cantor at the age of eight.

Eddie Becomes an Entertainer

Conditions in New York were bad and jobs were hard to find. Eddie wanted to be an actor. One of his friends suggested that he should go on the Amateur Show. He would get a dollar even if his act was a failure.

Eddie hesitated, but not for long, because a dollar was a lot of money at that time. He needed the money to buy food. Thus, at sixteen years of age, Eddie stepped on his first real stage. He did impersonations of local politicians and of famous actors whom he had never even seen. He did imitations of everybody he could think of. The audience was delighted. After the last performer had his turn, everyone came back on stage. The one who got the most applause won five dollars. When Eddie came out the people began to whistle, stamp their feet, and cheer. He was a hit. He won five dollars.

Eddie Cantor went on to appear in many Broadway musical comedies. He was on radio for many years. When television became popular Eddie was one of its greatest performers.

Helping Others

The really important part of this story does not concern Eddie Cantor's successful show business career. Nor is it about how wealthy he became. What is important is what he did with his talent and with the money he made.

When Eddie Cantor was thirty-seven years old, in 1929, he decided to retire. He wanted to devote all his time to his family of five daughters and his wife, Ida, who had been his childhood sweetheart. He wanted to devote his talents to charitable causes. Unfortunately, there was a stock market crash and Eddie Cantor lost all his money. Instead of retiring, he continued to work. But he did what he would have done if he had retired. He began to give benefit performances. Organizations which were raising money for charitable causes sold tickets and he came to sing, dance, and tell stories. Then he gave a little speech about why people should give more money to these causes. He didn't get paid for these shows.

Eddie Cantor made many friends along the way. He went all over the country to raise money for good causes. He raised over $60 million for Israel during and after World War II. He raised money for hospitals and research

The March of Dimes

President Franklin Roosevelt once sent for Eddie Cantor. He asked him to raise money for research to find a cure for polio. Eddie agreed. On his Sunday night radio program, he asked every person in the United States to send a dime to the White House to help fight

Eddie and his wife Ida.

the disease. That's how the March of Dimes started. By Tuesday the White House was flooded with envelopes containing coins. Years later Dr. Jonas Salk discovered his polio vaccine. His research was made possible by the March of Dimes.

The Stage Door Canteen

During World War II people from the entertainment industry decided to open the Stage Door Canteen. It was a place where men and women in the armed forces could go for free food, entertainment, and dancing. The sponsors of the Canteen wanted servicemen and servicewomen to have a good time without having to pay anything. The problem was where to get enough food. Eddie Cantor went to the big restaurants in New York and got them to donate food. He provided the milk himself. For eight months Eddie paid $600 a month to keep the soldiers and sailors supplied with fresh milk at the Stage Door Canteen. Just before he moved to California, he looked for someone else to donate the milk. The generous milk dealer who took over had been one of the poor, undernourished boys sent to Surprise Lake Camp by Eddie's club.

The Red Cross

In the early 1950s there was a shortage of blood in the Red Cross Blood Bank. Eddie Cantor was asked if he would help get blood donors. He agreed to do ten one-man shows in ten different cities. In order to get into the show a person had to donate a pint of blood. Eddie Cantor collected 110,000 pints of blood for the Red Cross.

Eddie Cantor and Al Jolson rehearsing for a benefit performance.

Eddie Cantor's Outstanding Achievements

For Eddie's sixty-fifth birthday a big party was organized in a hotel in Miami Beach, Florida. Two thousand people from all over the country came. Former President Harry Truman was the guest speaker. Nat King Cole, Jimmy Durante, George Jessel, Jack Benny, and many other movie and television stars entertained. It was a spectacular affair, but the presents were not for Eddie Cantor. They were for the State of Israel, one of his favorite causes. More than $15,450,000 was raised that night.

Eddie Cantor was a man who saw that money was needed for worthy causes. He realized that people enjoyed being entertained. He combined his talent for making people happy and his desire to help good causes. In the twenty-five years that he gave benefits, he raised $280,000,000. This money was for hospitals, camps, medical research—Catholic and Protestant causes as well as Jewish ones. By doing this, Eddie felt, he was showing his appreciation to the people who had cared enough when he was a small boy in need. He, too, cared about others, and wanted to help those who were in need.

Some old friends help Eddie celebrate his thirty-third wedding anniversary, 1947. *Left to right*: George Burns, Groucho Marx, Jack Benny, and Eddie.

TEST YOURSELF

Complete the following sentences with the words listed below:

1. Eddie Cantor went to _____ _____ _____.
2. His _____ raised him from the time he was two years old.
3. He and _____ _____ friends formed a club to help other boys go to camp.
4. The first time Eddie Cantor was on a real stage was in an _____ _____.
5. A performance for a charitable cause is called a _____.
6. The Salk vaccine was developed with money raised by the _____ of _____.
7. Eddie gave many shows to raise money for the _____ ____ _____
8. He helped supply the _____ _____ _____ with milk.
9. Cantor helped get 110,000 pints of blood for the _____ _____ _____

    March of Dimes   Surprise Lake Camp
    Amateur show   Twenty-nine
    Grandmother   American Red Cross
    Stage Door Canteen   State of Israel
    Benefit

QUOTATIONS

How do the following quotations relate to the story of Eddie Cantor?

Discuss them with your teacher.

"Care of the poor is incumbent on society as a whole."
                                              BENEDICT SPINOZA

"Nobody is ever impoverished through giving charity."
                                              MAIMONIDES

"He who is charitable and just fills the world with kindness."
                                              TALMUD: Sukka 49b

"Good men need no monuments: their deeds are their shrines."
                                              MISHNA: Shekalim

"The man who has led a good life will find many allies."
                                              NACHMAN OF BRATISLAV

IDEAS OF VALUE

Think about this:

Eddie Cantor was a poor boy growing up on the Lower East Side of New York. As a small child he was sent to a summer camp by a Jewish charity. That was probably the greatest influence in his life. Cantor had a real talent for entertaining people and making them happy. After he became a success in show business he realized that "Care of the poor is incumbent on society as a whole" (Spinoza, *Ethics*). He began to give shows to raise money for good causes. He got involved in helping people in many ways. "He who is charitable and just fills the world with kindness" (Talmud: *Sukka* 49b). Eddie Cantor filled the world with kindness by his support of the camp, the Stage Door Canteen, the March of Dimes, Bonds for Israel, the United Jewish Appeal, and many, many other organizations.

There are people in your community who are poor, sick, lonely, and friendless. You don't have money to give them. Besides, money won't solve all their problems. What can you do to show that you care? How can you become involved in helping them?

PUZZLE

To find the answer, add and subtract the letters in the names of the objects shown here. Keep each letter in its proper order.

By the time you reach the = sign you will have a word which tells what Eddie Cantor felt.

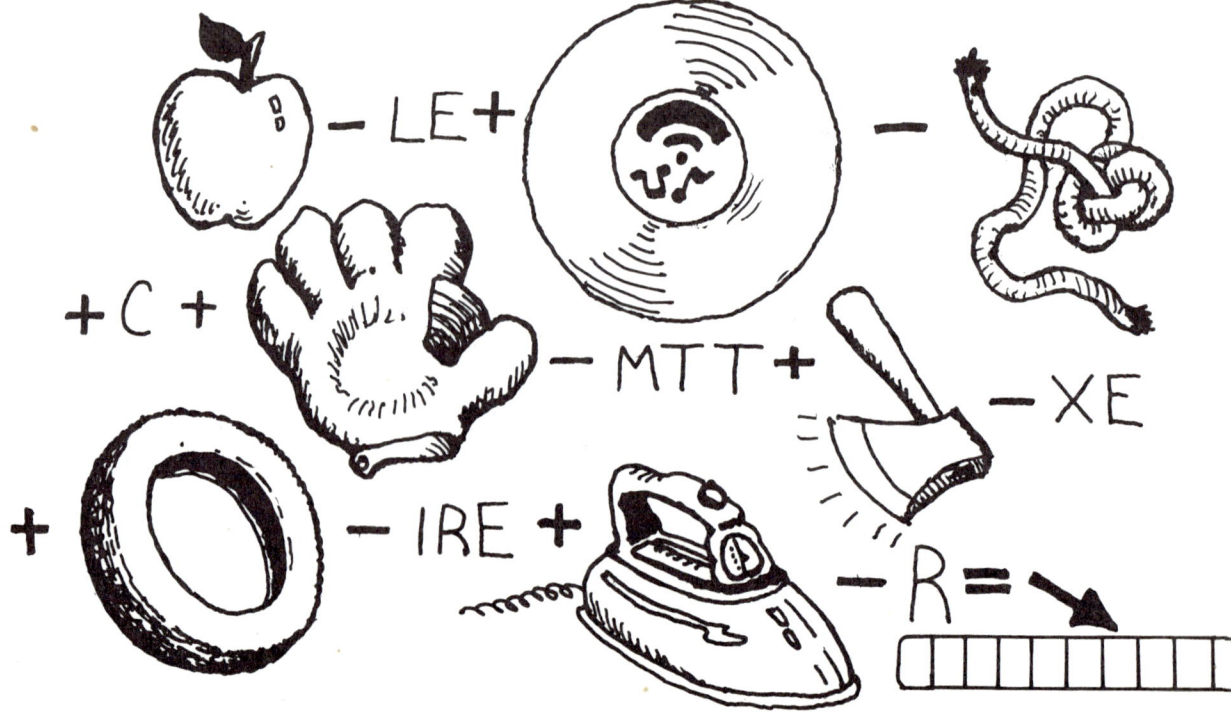

Eddie Cantor was a great comedian. He brought much laughter and happiness into the lives of many people. Eddie Cantor's personality also had a serious side. Eddie was a concerned human being and a dedicated Jew. He became involved in many good causes.

Are there any situations in your family, school, community, or synagogue which call for concern? Name a situation.

Would you be willing to turn your concern into action?

How would you go about becoming involved?

MOE BERG

The Smart Baseball Player

1902-1972

A Boy Who Loved Baseball

Morris Berg, known to the world as Moe, was born in 1902. His father and mother came to the United States from Russia after the pogroms in 1894. It was not safe for Jews living in Russia at that time. Some of those who could raise $10 for the boat fare escaped to America. When they arrived it was not easy for them to earn a living. The Bergs tried many things, including running a laundry. All the time he was ironing shirts, Bernard, the father, studied pharmacy. When he graduated he opened a drug store. His wife, Rose, also worked very hard so that they could establish themselves in this country. They had two sons. One became a doctor. The other one was Moe.

From the time Moe was three years old he was playing baseball. The patrolman who policed their street used to play catch with him. By the time Moe was seven he was drafted by his first team. It was a Methodist Church team, and the local paper ran a story about the game and how he won it for them.

Moe Becomes Interested in Languages

The family was living in Newark, New Jersey, which was a city with many immigrants. By the time Moe was in high school he began to show talents other than playing baseball. He had a remarkable ear for languages. He also wanted to know where words came from. He was interested in how words developed in other languages.

Moe applied to Princeton University and was admitted with the first class after World War I. At the university he became a star baseball player as well as a star student. Although he had many friends he was known as a loner. He preferred to be by himself when he wasn't on the field or in a class. Sometimes he would use both of his talents at the same time. During a game he would call signals to his teammates in Latin and confuse the other team. The opponents never knew who was going to field the ball. Moe graduated from Princeton with highest honors. His friends thought he was the smartest student in the class.

The Princeton baseball team of 1921. Moe Berg is in the second row, second from the right.

Major League Ballplayer

Immediately after his last college game, in 1923, the Brooklyn Dodgers signed Moe Berg on to their team. He was very pleased with this but wanted more than anything to continue his education. He wanted to go to Paris to study languages at the Sorbonne. One of his advisers suggested that he could do both. With some of the money he earned as a player he could go to France in the off-season. That's what Moe did. He was able to fulfill both ambitions. He played for many teams and in many positions. Eventually he became a catcher. When the sportswriters learned more about Moe they began to refer to him as "the Professor."

In 1926 Moe Berg didn't show up for spring training. His friends were amazed because they knew he loved to play the game. Soon they found out that he was back in school. This time he went to Columbia University Law School. The team owner told Berg he'd have to make a choice—either play baseball or go to school. Moe wanted to play but also wanted to learn. It was a difficult choice. He went to see one of his professors at the Law School about another problem. It was Moe's good fortune that the man whom he consulted was a sports fan.

When the professor realized that Moe was the same Berg who had played for Princeton, he made it possible for Moe to double up his classes so he would be available for spring training.

Moe Berg was a very unusual ball player. Tall and handsome, he had excellent manners, dressed well, and was a good conversationalist. People loved to talk to him and they listened to what he had to say. When he played for the Washington team he often spent his evenings with ambassadors from foreign countries. They were charmed by the fact that he could speak their languages. He made many friends during those years. He also learned a great deal about what was going on in other countries. All this was to be very useful later on.

Moe Berg in his catcher's uniform.

A Visit to Japan

In October 1934, Moe sailed for the Orient with an American League team that included players like Babe Ruth, Lou Gehrig, and Lefty Gomez. They were going to Japan to play the best Japanese college teams. They also were to encourage the Japanese to start a baseball league. By this time Moe Berg could speak Japanese like a native. This was his second trip to Japan. He made many friends there and gave lectures in Japanese. In addition to talking about baseball he used the opportunity to promote greater friendship between Japan and America. Many Japanese scholars asked his advice about teaching English to their students. He was very helpful to them. While Moe was in Tokyo, he photographed the city from the roof of a very tall building. During World War II, United States Military Intelligence used Moe's pictures in planning the massive air raids against Tokyo.

Contributions to the War Effort

Moe Berg was always a mysterious character when he was not on the ball field. None of his friends knew where he was between games or seasons. They knew that he traveled a great deal and knew many people in Washington. They even suspected that he might be some

Moe Berg during an instructional session at Waseda University, Tokyo, in 1932.

Opening day game for the White Sox in 1929 at Comiskey Park, Chicago. Moe Berg is the fifth from the left.

kind of spy. They didn't question him because they knew he wouldn't tell them even if it were so.

As it happened, while he was still playing major league baseball Moe visited Germany. It was 1933. One night he went to a place about five miles from the French border. He came to a large barn. Very quietly he opened the door and looked in. He found German fighter planes hidden there. The next morning he reported this to the American and French governments. He made and reported many other such discoveries. Since he knew and spoke so many languages, he was able to pick up useful information in the newspapers and at parties and meetings.

A month after the Japanese attacked Pearl Harbor, Moe Berg officially resigned from baseball and accepted an assignment to go to South America with a Good Will Mission. He had been studying the influence of enemy propaganda in the countries of Central and South America. He knew that the Germans were sending money to newspaper editors and radio station owners. The Nazis wanted them to believe that the United States was not their friend. Something had to be done to counteract this.

The American Air Force used bases in South America. Moe Berg wanted to be sure that the U.S. servicemen at these bases were treated well. He recommended that the soldiers be taught the language of the country where they were stationed. This would lead to better relations and more understanding. He also suggested that the officials who went to these countries should be friendly. Every effort should be made to assure the Latin Americans that the United States wanted to be a good neighbor.

Moe Berg on a secret scientific mission in Switzerland.

Moe Berg and the Atom Bomb

After he completed the Latin American Good Will tour Moe Berg went back to Europe. He wanted to find out what progress Germany's scientists were making with the development of the atomic bomb. He studied physics to learn all he could about atoms and uranium and all the other details of the bomb. He had secret meetings with the greatest scientists in Europe, then put together all the available information and sent his findings to the U.S. government. He urged the government to speed up the work being done in America. If Germany got the bomb first, he warned, the whole world would be destroyed.

Moe felt that all the top men in the field of atomic research should be encouraged to go to the United States. Many scientists were willing. The big question was how to get them out of their war-torn countries. Moe urged the President to arrange for them to be smuggled in and hidden. The President agreed. Many top experts were saved from Hitler and were able to help the Allies win the war.

While he was gathering scientific information, Moe Berg also kept the government informed about the war crimes that were being committed in the German-occupied territories. He reported on the tortures and atrocities the Germans were carrying on. He was so distressed by what he saw that he and some other men went to see the Pope. Moe spoke to the Pope in Italian, pleading with him to help save the Jews. Unfortunately, he didn't have any success.

As the war drew to a close, Moe appealed to the United States government to bring other European scientists to this country. Even those who were assistants on projects could make a contribution, he felt. His advice was not taken. After Germany surrendered, the Russians rounded up many of the remaining scientists. These scientists helped Russia to get ahead of the United States in the space race after the war.

Thanks to Moe Berg's help, the United States was able to develop the first atomic bomb. That shortened the war. Moe risked his life many times in order to get the needed information and pass it on to the proper authorities.

Sometimes one person who is willing to do dangerous things can save the lives of people he doesn't even know. Moe Berg, realizing the danger to his country and his people, was willing to take the necessary risks. With his help the war was shortened and thousands of lives were saved.

PUZZLE

By substituting a letter of the alphabet for a number you will spell out a description of Moe Berg.

13 15 18 18 9 19 2 5 18 7   23 1 19

1   13 1 10 15 18   12 5 1 7 21 5

2 1 19 5 2 1 12 12   16 12 1 25 5 18

1 14 4   1   19 16 25   6 15 18   20 8 5

21 14 9 20 5 4   19 20 1 20 5 19.

TEST YOURSELF

Are the following statements TRUE or FALSE?

1. Moe Berg was a lawyer. T__ F__
2. He spoke only English. T__ F__
3. The sportswriters called Berg "the Professor" because he was very smart. T__ F__
4. In Europe he helped spy on Nazi atomic bomb development. T__ F__
5. He saved the lives of many foreign scientists by getting them out of Europe. T__ F__
6. Moe Berg loved baseball and played catcher for several major league teams. T__ F__
7. When Moe went to see the Pope to plead with him to save the Jews, he spoke to him in Italian. T__ F__
8. In college Moe was a star player for Harvard. T__ F__

QUOTATIONS

How do the following quotations relate to the story of Moe Berg?

Discuss them with your teacher.

"Learning is more important than action—when it leads to action."
TALMUD: Megillah 26

"A man should never stop learning, even on his last day."
MAIMONIDES

"The intelligent will know his time, guard his tongue, and attend to his business."
SOLOMON IBN GABIROL, Mibhar Ha-Peninim

"Knowledge and action are twins, they glorify each other."
JOSEPH KIMHI, Shekel Hakadosh

"In critical times men can save their lives only by risking them."
LÉON BLUM, For All Mankind

IDEAS OF VALUE

Think about this:

Moe Berg was an unusual baseball player and an unexpected spy. At college he was an excellent student. He had a very good ear for foreign languages. When he went to Japan with a baseball team he managed to take pictures which later helped the United States government. "In critical times men can save their lives only by risking them" (Léon Blum, *For All Mankind*). Moe Berg went to Europe during World War II to find out how far the Germans had gotten with the development of the atomic bomb. He also kept the American government informed about Nazi war crimes. He risked his life many times to get this information. Moe Berg was always considered a "loner" by his friends and teammates. They didn't know how he spent his time, but they guessed it had something to do with his great ability as a scholar. "The intelligent will know his time, guard his tongue, and attend to his business" (Ibn Gabirol, *Mibhar Ha-Peninim*). They would have been surprised to know that Moe Berg was devoting his life to keeping his country and his people free.

As a citizen of this country you expect to have certain rights and freedoms. Among these are free speech, freedom of religion, a free press, the right to vote, and the right to an education. If you had to give up one of these, which would you choose? Why? Which would you be willing to fight for at the risk of your life? Why?

Moe Berg was a professional spy and placed his life in great danger. Berg put his life on the line so that America could preserve its freedom. Liberty has long been important to Jews. The Liberty Bell in Philadelphia has a biblical quotation inscribed on it: "Proclaim liberty throughout the land."

We in America have our freedoms guaranteed to us by the Constitution. What do these freedoms mean to you?

freedom of speech,

freedom of the press,

freedom of religion,

freedom of assembly,

the right to vote,

other,

RABBI LEO BAECK

The Keeper of his People

1873–1956

To the Germans he was #187,894. To the Jews and Christians in the concentration camp he was teacher, rabbi, friend, and spiritual guide. His name was Leo Baeck. He was the leader of the Jewish community in Berlin when Hitler came to power. This was a responsibility he took very seriously.

The Nazi Persecution of the Jews

Hitler made the Germans believe that their poverty and unemployment were caused by the Jews. Much like the Russians at the end of the nineteenth century, they blamed the Jews for all their troubles. The German people needed somebody to blame for their misfortunes. Who better than the Jews!

They expelled all the Jewish children from the schools. Then they began to take Jewish property away. Many Jews were sent to prison for no reason. Although Jews had been living in Germany for a thousand years, they were treated like outsiders. At first, many of them did not believe that they would be mistreated. They had made so many contributions to the progress of the country.

Rabbi Leo Baeck as a chaplain in the German Army during World War I.

They were good citizens. They were patriotic. No one would bother them. That's what they thought. The Germans thought otherwise. No Jew, no matter how un-Jewish, was exempt from the terrible treatment which the Nazis dreamed up.

Jews were rounded up like cattle and taken to concentration camps. A number was tattooed on each person's arm in order to make the Jews lose their identity and feel like non-persons.

On the night of November 9, 1938, the Nazis destroyed all the synagogues in Germany. They smashed the windows, tore the Torah scrolls, and set fire to them. In some places they locked people in the building while they burned it down. It was a night which is still remembered as Kristallnacht— "the night of the broken glass."

A Rabbi Resists the Nazis

After the synagogues were destroyed Rabbi Baeck began to hold services in cellars or attics, or even the kitchen of an empty restaurant. When the Nazis discovered this they arrested Rabbi Baeck. They arrested him five times, but each time they let him go because many people outside of Germany knew this great scholar and were concerned about his safety.

Rabbi Baeck had several chances to save himself from the Nazis. A community in the United States offered him a congregation in America, but he declined the offer. Another time, after bribing German officials, he took a trainload of children to Holland. He could have stayed there in safety, but he returned to Germany. When he took a group of children to England he was again offered a chance to stay. Again he refused. His people in Germany needed him. As long as one Jew remained there, he would be there too.

In the Concentration Camp

In 1943 Leo Baeck was arrested again. This time the world was at war. Now it was safe to send the great man to a concentration camp. No one could do anything about it. He was sent to Theresienstadt.

There Rabbi Baeck was offered a special job. If he kept the guards informed about what the prisoners were doing, he would be given special privileges and better food. He refused. He would not

A synagogue which was destroyed during "Kristallnacht."

help the Germans in any way. He would not allow himself to be singled out as someone special. He preferred to be among the people as their friend.

Rabbi Baeck was assigned the task of a horse. They put a yoke around his neck and shoulders and had him pull the garbage wagon up and down the muddy streets of the camp. Fortunately for him, the wagon needed two horses. His partner was another scholar. So the two men pulled the wagon and discussed literature and philosophy. The rabbi's spirit remained unbroken. Instead, he learned to look forward to these discussions in spite of the hard work.

It was against the rules to teach in the concentration camps. Dr. Baeck organized secret classes. Every night the subject was different. No matter how tired he was, and no matter how tired and hungry the people were, they went to the lecture. If anyone was caught the penalty was death. This didn't stop them. They had people who acted as lookouts. They signaled when a guard was coming and then everything stopped. This was the way Rabbi Baeck

A "relocation center."

Deportation of Jews to the concentration camp.

helped his fellow prisoners to keep sane. Thanks to his efforts, they continued to be civilized people no matter what the Nazis did.

A Close Call from Death

When an inmate didn't do enough work, or was too sick or too tired to be useful, the Nazis sent that inmate to Auschwitz. It meant certain death to be shipped out. Leo Baeck helped as many as he could to avoid this fate. He stayed with those who were ill. He encouraged them to stay on their feet. When people were dying, Rabbi Baeck was called. He comforted them, just as he had done when he was a rabbi in Berlin. He sometimes took an extra piece of bread from a healthy person and gave it to a sick one. When people lost hope, he kept them from throwing themselves at the cruel guards. As one man he helped save the lives of many others.

By a stroke of luck, he was never sent to Auschwitz. It was discovered by accident that he was still alive. Adolph Eichmann, one of the most hated of all the Nazi leaders, came to Theresienstadt one day. He recognized the "horse" pulling the garbage wagon. Long before, he had given orders that Dr. Baeck was to be sent with a carload of prisoners to be killed. When the name Baeck was called, another man, whose name was Beck, answered. He was deported and the rabbi never knew that he himself had been marked for the gas chamber. When Eichmann realized what had happened, he put Leo Baeck's name on the list for the next shipment. This was in 1945, toward the end of the war. Before the Eichmann order could be carried out, Russian soldiers reached the camp.

Free at Last

The Russians arrested the German guards and rounded up the camp inmates. Knowing how much they hated the guards, the Russians told the prisoners they could do whatever they wanted to them. A few prisoners stepped forward to take their revenge. Rabbi Baeck stopped them. He would not allow them to sink so low, he said. That would be permitting the Germans to accomplish what they set out to do. That would destroy the Jews as a civilized people. The rabbi explained that it

Rabbi Leo Baeck

would be better to bring these cruel monsters to trial before the entire world. Then the world would learn that such evil would not go unpunished.

A month later an American came to the camp to take Rabbi Baeck out of that miserable place. Again he refused to leave. He said that he would be ready to go in about a month, for by then all the other Jews would be well enough to leave. A month later he was taken to London. Once again he was a free man. Although he was seventy-five years old he still felt that he had work to do.

In London Leo Baeck was elected president of the World Union for Progressive Judaism. Once again he was serving his people. He was invited to

The Nazis forced the Jews to wear yellow stars as a sign of shame. This is the yellow star worn by Rabbi Leo Baeck.

teach at the Hebrew Union College in Cincinnati, Ohio. There he was very much loved by the students, many of whom are the Reform rabbis of today.

Leo Baeck was born in 1873, the son of a German rabbi. He died in 1956, having influenced the lives of thousands of people all over the world. One man gave courage to hundreds of others during the worst period in the world's history. At the risk of his own life, he helped others to live with dignity. He taught the value of human life when others wanted to destroy it. He knew the importance of each person in a world where no one seemed to matter. Always, he was part of the community.

The rabbinical seminary in Berlin. Rabbi Leo Baeck taught in this school.

PUZZLE

BREAK THE CODE

Find the correct "A" and all the other letters will follow. For example, YZVXP spells the name of the hero of this story.

OVL YZVXP DZMGVW
GSV QVDH GL IVNZRM
XRERORAVW VEVM RU
GSVRI XZKGLIH YVSZEVW
ORPV YVZHGH.

TEST YOURSELF

Which of the following statements are true and which are false? Check the correct space.

1. Leo Baeck was the chief rabbi of Berlin. T__ or F__
2. The Nazis liked Rabbi Baeck. T__ or F__
3. All the synagogues in Germany were destroyed on Kristallnacht. T__ or F__
4. Rabbi Baeck could have saved himself several times. T__ or F__
5. He conducted services after the synagogues were destroyed. T or F__
6. Rabbi Baeck was known as the teacher of Theresienstadt. T__ or F__
7. Rabbi Baeck allowed the Jews to take revenge on the German guards after the war. T__ or F__
8. It was important for the people in the concentration camps to know who they were. T__ or F__
9. After the war Rabbi Baeck was elected president of the World Union for Progressive Judaism. T__ or F__

QUOTATIONS

How do the following quotations relate to the story of Rabbi Leo Baeck?

Discuss them with your teacher.

"Who train themselves in wisdom cultivate true courage."
PHILO, Virtues

"Is not the chief function of our religion to engender in us a sense of human worth?"
JONATHAN EYBESHITZ, Yaarot Debash

"Poverty, sickness, and terror are easier to bear with faith."
SOLOMON IBN GABIROL, Mibhar Ha-Peninim

"A teacher should cherish his pupils as much as himself."
MEKILTA: Exodus 18:9

"All men are responsible for one another."
TALMUD: Sanhedrin 27b

IDEAS OF VALUE

Think about this:

Rabbi Leo Baeck learned from the *Ethics of the Fathers* that it is important for a person not to separate himself or herself from the community. When Hillel, in *Pirke Avoth* 11:5, said: "Separate not yourself from the congregation," he meant that a person should not try to be an exception. One should not try to gain special favors by being singled out. Rather, one should stay with the others in the group and be an equal in all treatment.

In school the principal calls you into the office and offers you tickets to a basketball or football game, or even better grades than you earned so that you can get a better report card. All you have to do in return is tell the principal who has been violating the honor system and cheating on tests. You would like to go to the game but haven't the money for a ticket. You also haven't been doing as well as you should in math. Would you accept the offer? Explain the reasons for your answer.

Leo Baeck was a rabbi who would accept no special treatment. He was offered an opportunity to save himself from the concentration camp. Rabbi Baeck refused to leave the Jews of Germany.

A shepherd belongs with his flock; and a rabbi belongs with his people.

What qualities do you admire in Rabbi Leo Baeck? You too have qualities which people respect. Describe some of your qualities on the scrolls and awards. Describe some of your friend's qualities

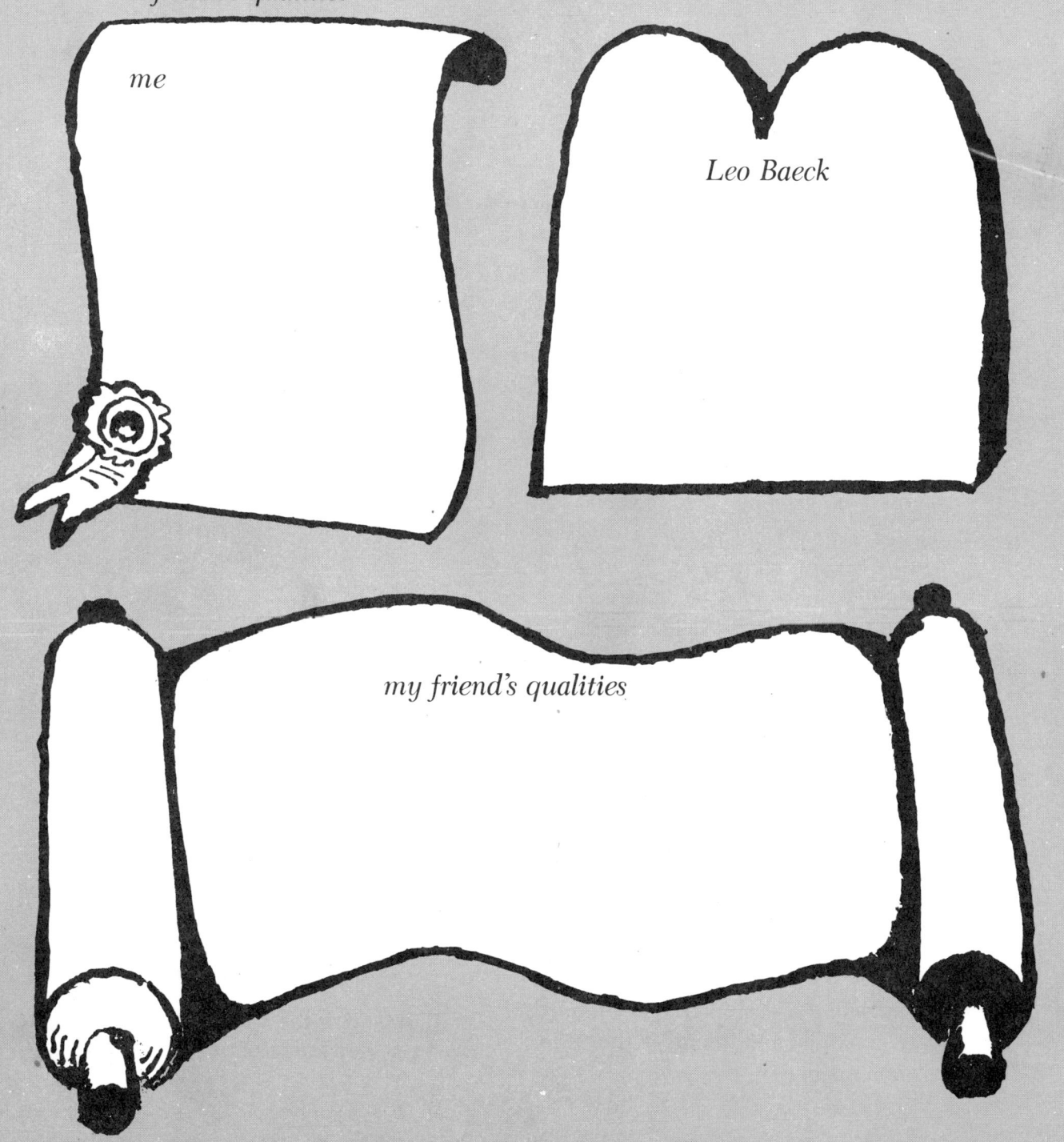

DAVID SARNOFF

The Great Communicato

1891-1971

An Immigrant Youth

What do the sinking of the *Titanic* and a wireless station on top of a New York skyscraper have in common? David Sarnoff. Who was David Sarnoff He was the son of a poor house painter who was brought to this country when he was nine years old. That was in 1900.

David Sarnoff helped to support his family by selling newspapers and delivering packages. Later he became a messenger. He was very interested in Morse code, so he saved his money and bought a telegraph instrument to practice sending messages. Somebody suggested that he try to get a job as a telegrapher at the Marconi Wireless Telegraph Company. When David went there the only opening was for a messenger. He decided to take the job. At least he would be around if the other position opened up.

David Sarnoff at the age of nineteen, when he was a wireless operator on the S.S. *Beothic*.

A Sailor's Life Is Saved

At seventeen David Sarnoff became a telegrapher on a lonely island off the New England coast. He was delighted because he would be doing what he liked best. He stayed there only a short time. Then he became the first wireless operator on a ship bound for Alaska. One day he received a message from a ship about a hundred miles away. A sailor was seriously ill and they had no doctor aboard. They needed help. Sarnoff told the doctor on his ship about the message. The doctor prescribed the treatment over the wireless and the man recovered. David Sarnoff helped save a life by his quick response and his clever use of the ships radio. As a result the Marine Medico Service was formed. If someone becomes ill aboard a ship which has no doctor, help can be gotten quickly by using the radio.

David decided he would like more education in engineering. He got a transfer to a station in Brooklyn, New York, where he was able to go to school in his free time. While he was going to school he became a wireless operator for the Marconi station on top of one of New York's tall buildings.

The Night the *Titanic* Went Down

On the night of April 14, 1912, David Sarnoff was on duty at the wireless station. The S. S. *Titanic* was on its way to New York. It was the luxury liner's first voyage. Aboard the ship the passengers were having a big party. The crew on deck were unable to see very much because it was a dark night. Suddenly, the ship shook, knocking many of the dancers at the party off balance. The men outside were knocked to the deck. For a few moments no one knew what had happened. Many of the people panicked. The ship had hit an iceberg. There was a big hole in the hull and water was pouring in. The ship was sinking. The radio operator sent out an SOS.

David Sarnoff heard it. He notified other ships in the area that help was needed. The S. S. *Carpathia* went to the rescue of the *Titanic* and was able to save some of the people. Then they wired David the names of those they were able to rescue. He notified the families, who were anxiously awaiting the news. David Sarnoff stayed on duty for seventy-two hours. As a result of this incident, Congress passed a law which required any ship carrying more than fifty people to install a radio.

Radio and TV Executive

Sarnoff became more and more important in the Marconi company. His opinions were respected. He was the first one who saw the possibilities of having radios in homes. He sent a memo to the president of the company telling him of the idea. The company soon began to produce radio "music boxes"—what we know today as the radio.

David Sarnoff using the telegraph key on his desk.

Planning for D-Day with one of Eisenhower's staff.

In 1919, when the Marconi company became part of a new company called Radio Corporation of America, Sarnoff was given an executive job. He developed the idea of a network of radio stations across the country. Later, he extended this idea to television. Through the networks David Sarnoff was the first one to broadcast national coverage of political conventions, college football games, major league baseball, and prize fights. He was the first one to arrange for the opera to be heard directly from the Metropolitan Opera House in New York. He also introduced the first news broadcasts. By 1930 Sarnoff was president of RCA. Through his work and foresight the public was made aware of the value of radio. He was also instrumental in furthering the development of television. In 1944 the Television Broadcasters Association gave him the title of "Father of American Television."

David Sarnoff rose from messenger boy to president of one of the largest corporations in this country. He never forgot his people. He gave a great deal of his time and money to Jewish causes. Although he came to America as a young boy, he always remembered that his father left Russia because Jews were persecuted there.

During World War II David Sarnoff saw the same thing happening in Germany and the rest of Central Europe. He volunteered his tremendous talents to help the Allies win the war. He became a brigadier general and served as Chief Communications Consultant to General Dwight D. Eisenhower. Even though he was accepted by all people he remembered that he was a Jew.

David Sarnoff realized the important contribution communications could make towards greater understanding in the world. He devoted his life to helping us all enjoy music, news, sporting events, and drama.

David Sarnoff

PUZZLE

David Sarnoff made great contributions to the world's method of

```
              C _ _ _
        _ _ _ _ O _ _
              M _ _ _ _ _ _ _
              M _ _ _ _ _
            _ U _ _ _ _ _ _
        _ _ _ _ N _ _
            _ I _ _ _ _ _ _
            _ C _ _ _ _ _
              _ _ A
              T _ _ _ _ _ _ _ _
        _ _ _ _ I _
        _ _ _ _ O
              N _ _ _
```

From the words below select those which will fit correctly to form the word describing David Sarnoff's area of interest.

| MUSIC BOX | TITANIC | RUSSIA | MESSENGER | MARCONI | NEWS |
| MORSE | ICEBERG | WIRELESS | RCA RADIO | TELEVISION | CODE |

TEST YOURSELF

Underline the correct answer:

1. David Sarnoff helped support his family by (a) singing on the stage, (b) working as a messenger boy, (c) building bridges.

2. He developed a great interest in (a) Morse code, (b) batting averages, (c) girls.

3. He was the first wireless operator on a ship going to (a) Tahiti, (b) Russia, (c) Alaska.

4. He helped a sick sailor on another ship by (a) using the wireless, (b) prescribing two aspirins, (c) suggesting he have some chicken soup.

5. Later, Sarnoff became the wireless operator (a) in Disneyland, (b) on top of a tall building, (c) in a movie house.

6. When the *Titanic* hit an iceberg David Sarnoff received (a) the SOS, (b) some ice cubes, (c) a letter telling him about it.

7. He stayed on duty at the station (a) an hour, (b) a week, (c) 72 hours.

8. Congress passed a law that ships with more than (a) 50, (b) 2, (c) 5 people aboard had to have a radio transmitter.

9. During World War II Sarnoff was (a) a private, (b) a sailor, (c) a brigadier general.

10. He made it possible to broadcast (a) news, (b) baseball games, (c) political conventions.

IDEAS OF VALUE

Think about this:

From the time he was a young boy David Sarnoff worked. "By the sweat of your brow you shall eat bread" (Bible: Genesis 3:19). He did many things in order to earn money and help support his family. Even though he worked hard he developed some of his own interests. "To have a trade is to have a fence: it protects you . . . " (Tosephta: *Kiddushin* 1:11). He became a skillful telegrapher. He was able to help some of the people on the *Titanic* by sending radio messages to and from the sinking ship. It was through his talent and his trade that he was later able to expand the whole field of communications.

You will have to make a choice of a career sometime in the near future. You may want to learn a trade or go into business. Perhaps you will choose to be a doctor or a lawyer. What do you think will influence you most when you make this decision? Will you expect immediate rewards from your job? Will you be willing to start at the bottom and work your way up? Why?

QUOTATIONS

How do the following quotations relate to the story of David Sarnoff?

Discuss them with your teacher.

"*The heroic hours of life do not announce their presence by drum or trumpet.*"
BENJAMIN CARDOZO

"*Knowledge shall be increased.*"
BIBLE: Daniel 12:4

"*When you do not know, do not be ashamed to admit it.*"
TALMUD: Derek Eretz 1:22

"*Our days are scrolls: write on them what you want to be remembered for.*"
BAHYA IBN PAQUDA, Duties of the Heart

"*Faith is not only in the heart; it should be put into words.*"
NACHMAN OF BRATISLAV

Life was not easy for David Sarnoff. He worked hard to develop his own trade and career.

Choose three careers you might wish to pursue. Rank your choices on the basis of prestige, salary, service, and Jewish commitment.

	CAREER I	CAREER II	CAREER III
prestige			
salary			
service			
Jewish commitment			

What career do you think you will choose?

What do you hope to achieve in your career?

List the talents and skills required for the career you expect to choose.

GOLDA MEIR

The Lady Who Was Prime Minister
1898–1977

Why a Little Girl Fasted

Golda was born in Russia in 1898. She was only four years old when she first learned what a pogrom was. Czar Nicholas, the country's ruler, kept the peasants very poor. Poor people are usually angry and want someone to blame for their poverty. The Czar made the peasants believe that the Jews were the cause of their troubles. When the peasants became drunk they rode through the Jewish neighborhoods killing people and destroying property. The police didn't do anything about it. They felt that the peasants were entitled to take their misery out on somebody. Who better than the Jews? Golda was only four years old when it almost happened in her town but she never forgot it.

When she was five years old there was a terrible pogrom in a city called Kishinev. A group of drunken peasants looted and burned down a store owned by Jews. The group turned into a mob. They burned more stores, and before the night was over forty-five Jews were dead. There was nothing anyone could do.

The people of Golda's town felt helpless. They were very upset by what had happened. They decided to fast as a way of showing their sympathy and grief. No

Jewish victims of the Kishinev pogrom

adult would eat or drink for twenty-four hours. It would be like Yom Kippur. That morning Golda didn't eat breakfast. Her mother was too upset to notice. By lunchtime she still hadn't eaten. Her mother urged her but she refused. Little Golda knew that people were suffering, and even though she was so young, she felt that she, too, had to be part of her people.

The Family Moves to America

Golda's father saw that the situation in Russia was getting worse. He decided to go to America. He would work and save enough money to send for the rest of the family. In the meantime they would remain in Russia.

Golda's older sister was a member of a group which was planning a revolution against the government. That was a very dangerous thing to do. Almost every day more people were taken to jail and tortured by the police. They were trying to find out who else was involved. When Golda's mother learned that her daughter was one of the revolutionaries, she decided not to wait any longer. They would go to America at once. There was no legal way for them to leave the country because they had no passports. They had to rely on peasants who were willing to smuggle them across the border into Poland. From there they traveled a long time by wagon until they reached Antwerp, Belgium. There, they took a small boat to America. The voyage took about a month. At last they came to Milwaukee, Wisconsin, where their father was living. In the fall the children started school. This was a very happy time for Golda.

Books for Needy Children

School in Milwaukee was free but the textbooks cost money. Some of the children were very poor. They had to stand up in class and say that they couldn't afford to buy books. Then they were given old books. Golda was outraged at this procedure. She could not stand to see people embarrassed because they were poor. She gathered her friends together and told them she had a plan. They would go from door to door in the neighborhood to raise money to buy books for the poor children.

At first Golda's friends didn't want to do it. They said it was just like begging. She replied that begging, if it's for a good cause, is all right. In a few days the girls had collected enough money to buy a large stack of books, but Golda began to worry about what would happen when the books were all gone.

Soon she came up with another plan. She and her friends would hire a hall and give a show to raise money. Again, her friends hesitated. Who would want to watch a bunch of fourth-graders sing and dance and recite poems? Golda was very convincing and soon they agreed.

On the night of the performance all the girls participated, but the one who did the most was Golda. After the entertainment she got up and made a speech. She told her story simply. Children needed books. Books cost money. Many children didn't have the money to pay for the books. She asked the people in the audience to open their hearts and their pocketbooks. They were moved by her sincerity and did as she asked. Now, no more children would have to be embarrassed because they were too poor to afford the books they needed in school.

Golda Meir working on the Kibbutz at Merhavya, 1922.

Golda Becomes a Zionist

When Golda graduated she was the outstanding student in the class. She wanted to go on to high school and become a teacher. Golda's parents were very much against the idea. In Milwaukee, at that time, teachers were not allowed to be married. The thought of Golda remaining an old maid upset her parents, but Golda wanted to do something important with her life. Even though they objected, she went on to high school. She taught English to new immigrants for ten cents an hour in her spare time.

When Golda had enough money saved for a ticket she ran away to Denver, where her married sister was living. While she was there Golda made many friends. Among them was Morris Meyerson, a quiet man who rarely said very much. Unlike the other young people that Golda met, he was not interested in politics. His interest was in the arts, music, and literature. He and Golda fell in love.

Golda's parents finally realized that she was entitled to go to school if she wanted to. They wrote her a letter asking her to come home. She left Morris and her sister and returned to Milwaukee. She and Morris wrote to each other every day.

This happened at the time of World War I. The Russians and the Germans were fighting in the area where Golda was born. No matter who won the battles, the Jews always lost. They suffered because they were a persecuted minority. With each report from Europe, Golda became more convinced that the Jews of the world had to have a country of their own—a place where they would not be guests, a place they could call home. More and more she turned to Zionism and the idea of a Jewish homeland in Palestine. Golda made speeches whereever she found an audience. She spoke in synagogues, in union halls, and even on street corners.

Golda wanted to live in Palestine, but Morris wanted to stay in America. He came to Milwaukee and tried to convince her to give up her plans. What would she do in Palestine, in that desert? She wanted to be a farmer on a kibbutz. That wasn't for him. He went back to Denver. After a few months, though, Morris came back to Milwaukee. Golda and Morris were married in December 1917. In May 1921 they set sail from New York to Palestine. The trip took two months.

Golda's Life in Palestine

More than anything, now that she was in Palestine, Golda wanted to join a kibbutz. On a kibbutz everyone is equal. Everything is shared. Everyone has to work. Twice Golda and Morris were refused membership. The kibbutzniks said that an American girl was too soft for kibbutz life; as soon as things got really bad, the Americans would go back to America.

Golda refused to be discouraged. She applied again, and this time they were accepted. At last, Golda was a kibbutznik. She was very happy even though she had never worked so hard in her life, but Morris was unhappy. He missed the cultural life of the city. Finally, he convinced Golda that they should move to Jerusalem. There, their two children were born. Even with the children to keep her busy Golda felt as if she weren't really living. She was not making any contribution to the land.

Working to Help the Jewish State

One day, on her way home from the market, she met an old friend from the kibbutz. This was a very important meeting because it opened up a whole new phase of her life. She was offered a job taking charge of the Women's Labor Council. Her family wasn't very happy about it, but they soon learned how important it was for Golda to do this kind of work.

From then on Golda had one important job after another. She made valuable contributions to her people. Just before the Declaration of the State of Israel, for example, money was desperately needed for guns and ammunition. Everyone thought it would be impossible to get more money from the Jews of America. David Ben-Gurion, the head of the Jewish Agency, was enraged, but Golda volunteered to go to America.

At a large meeting in Chicago, Golda told her story. In her plain, direct way, she told about the young settlers and the well-armed Arabs who were attacking them. The Jews sometimes had to defend themselves with stones when they lacked guns and ammunition. But stones can't win a war. Guns and planes and tanks were needed. When she finished speaking she got a standing ovation. Everyone in the audience rose up and cheered her. By the time the afternoon was over Golda had pledges for almost $30,000,000. She traveled all over the United States in the next two and a half months, raising enormous sums of money. The money Golda raised was used to buy weapons for the Haganah.

Foreign Minister of the New State

On May 14, 1948, the State of Israel was proclaimed. Golda Meyerson was one of the signers of the Proclamation. The next day the Arabs attacked Israel in full force. Three days after the war started Golda was on her way back to the United States to raise more money. She raised the much-needed money and was preparing to leave for home when she received a telegram from Ben-Gurion, who was now the Israeli Prime Minister. He wanted her to be Israel's Ambassador to Russia. All the bad memories of her childhood in Russia came back to her. She would not go. She belonged home

In 1948 Golda Meir was appointed Israeli Ambassador to Russia. Here she presents her credentials to the Deputy Premier in Moscow.

with the people fighting the Arabs. But after she thought about it for a while, she agreed. In September 1948, she arrived in Moscow and opened the Embassy.

Golda ran the Embassy like a kibbutz. Everyone, including herself, took turns marketing and cooking. There was nothing fancy about it but diplomats from other countries loved to come visit them. On Rosh Hashanah the staff went to the synagogue. When the Jews of Moscow saw Golda they cheered. She was their connection with Jews outside of Russia. They were afraid to be too outspoken in their friendship because the Russian government did not believe in freedom of religion. If they were caught being too friendly they would be punished. That was a sad thing for Golda to realize.

In February 1949, the United Nations helped arrange a truce between Israel and the Arabs. Now, more than ever, Golda wanted to be back in Israel. She got her wish a few months later when she was asked to become Minister of Labor. Now she really felt that she could do something to help the people. New immigrants were arriving by the thousands. They needed homes and jobs. Golda was in charge of helping them. It was her task to make them into productive citizens. She created jobs for them. They learned how to build houses, construct roads, and work in factories. Later on, they learned to be farmers, business people, and teachers. Golda held this post for seven years.

Ben-Gurion then asked Golda to become Foreign Minister. The only catch was that she would have to adopt a Hebrew name. She and Morris had been separated for several years, but she hadn't wanted to change her name. Now she had no choice. She decided to use the Hebrew version closest to the original. She became Golda Meir, Foreign Minister of the State of Israel.

In 1964 she represented the Israeli government at the independence celebration for the new nation of Zambia. Southern Rhodesia, a neighboring country, invited the visiting diplomats to see Victoria Falls, the highest waterfall in the world. They were all anxious to go. When they arrived at the border between Rhodesia and Zambia, the

Golda Meir conferring with President Kennedy, 1962.

police asked them to form two lines, one for whites and one for blacks. Golda turned around and headed for the car which brought her. She would not be a party to discrimination between races. As she walked to her car she heard noise behind her. She turned to see what it was. All the diplomats were following her. None of them was willing to visit the Falls under those conditions. Golda was very popular among the diplomats. They liked her honesty and her warm feelings for people.

Even as a high official in the government Golda did things for herself. She didn't want servants to wait on her. In fact, many important government meetings were held in her kitchen, where she prepared tea for the other officials. Sometimes they were called Golda's "Kitchen Cabinet."

In 1966 Golda Meir was sixty-eight years old. She decided it was time to retire. Ben-Gurion had retired a few years earlier. She felt that she had earned a rest.

Golda Becomes Prime Minister

In February 1969, as Golda was driving from Jerusalem to Tel Aviv, she heard a news report on the radio. Prime Minister Levi Eshkol had died of a heart attack. She turned her car around and went back to Jerusalem. He had been her friend. She wanted to be with their other friends.

Now the government needed a new head. Elections weren't scheduled until the next fall. It was suggested that the Cabinet appoint someone temporarily, someone who was not really interested in keeping the job. The perfect person was Golda Meir. Although she was seventy years old, she was still very capable. So there she was, back in office again. She did such a wonderful job that she was elected and re-elected. She served for five years.

In 1973, on Yom Kippur Day, the Arabs again attacked the Jewish State. It was a bitter war with many casualties on both sides. Some people blamed the government for not being better prepared. Golda worked long and hard during the war. She flew to Washington to meet with President Nixon. Finally, a truce was arranged. Cease-fire lines were established. The war was over. In June 1974, Golda Meir retired again.

Golda's Life Ends

In November 1977, President Anwar Sadat of Egypt came to Jerusalem at the invitation of Prime Minister Menachem Begin. It was a very important breakthrough in the relations between Israel and Egypt. When Sadat was introduced to Golda he smiled graciously. They both knew that he had often referred to her as "that old lady." Now, face to face, they acted like friends. In fact, Golda Meir, herself a grandmother for many years, brought a gift for the Egyptian President's new grandchild.

Shortly after the eventful day in November Golda Meir died. She had suffered from cancer for ten years and no one knew about it. She had a job to do and she did it. That was the way she was. Her devotion to the development of a Jewish homeland in Israel was great. The Jews finally had a place where they were the majority. They did not have to depend upon other people for their freedom. Golda Meir, as much as anyone who ever lived, helped make this happen.

Golda Meir

Golda Meir with Mrs. Eleanor Roosevelt, 1956.

QUOTATIONS

How do the following quotations relate to the story of Golda Meir?

Discuss them with your teacher.

"Anti-Semitism diverts men from the real tasks confronting them. It diverts them from the true cause of their woes."
   JACQUES MARITAIN, A Christian Looks at the Jewish Question

"Anti-Semitism is not to be overcome by getting people to forget us, but to know us."
   MEYER LEVIN, In Search

"A homeland cannot be bought with money or conquered by the sword. It has to be created with one's own toil and sweat."
   DAVID BEN-GURION

"A Jewish life must have a Jewish land."
   SHEMARYA LEVIN, The Arena

"Words that come from the heart enter the heart."
   MOSES IBN EZRA, Shirat Yisrael

PUZZLE

Substitute letters of the alphabet for the numbers. You will decode a lesson which we can learn from the life of Golda Meir.

15 14 5   9 19   14 5 22 5 18   20 15 15   for example: O N E
25 15 21 14 7   14 15 18   20 15 15   15 14 5
15 12 4   20 15   13 1 11 5   1
3 15 14 20 18 9 2 21 20   9 15 14   20 15
19 15 3 9 5 20 25.

TEST YOURSELF

Choose the word or phrase that completes each of the following sentences.

1. A pogrom is _____
2. A revolution is _____
3. Asking for money is OK if _____
4. If a person wants to, he or she should be allowed to _____
5. Jews were persecuted because _____
6. In a kibbutz everyone is _____
7. When she asked for money Golda was _____
8. As Ambassador to Russia Golda Meir attended services and _____

a. they were a minority who refused to give up their religion and their traditions.

b. it is for a good cause.

c. an attack on Jews for no reason except that they are Jews.

d. encouraged the Jews who still remained in Moscow.

e. to overthrow the government by force.

f. equal.

g. choose his or her own career.

h. sincere and spoke simply.

IDEAS OF VALUE

Think about this:

As a young child in Russia Golda Meir was frightened by pogroms. Her family left Russia for safety. When they came to America Golda went to school in Milwaukee, Wisconsin, where her family lived. She started a fund to pay for books for poor children. "Shaming another in public is like shedding blood" (Talmud: *Baba Metzia* 58b). She wanted to save them the embarrassment of having to admit to being too poor to buy books. She studied to become a teacher. Before long she realized that the Jewish people needed a homeland of their own. She became a devoted Zionist. After World War I she moved to Palestine and lived on a kibbutz for a while. She became involved in developing the state in many ways. When the state was established she was one of the signers of the Proclamation. She was appointed Israel's first Ambassador to Russia. All her life she was against discrimination of any kind. "Are you not like the children of the Ethiopians to me, O children of Israel?" (Bible: Amos 9:7). She later became temporary Prime Minister but was so popular that she was re-elected five times. She retired from public office in 1974.

When you come to school the teacher tells all the children with blue eyes that they have to sit in the back of the room. When they go to lunch they have to sit in a certain section of the cafeteria. You have brown eyes. What would you do? Why did you decide that? What do you think Golda Meir would have done?

Golda Meir experienced pogroms in Russia. Her experiences made her into an active enemy of prejudice and segregation.

You, too, have been influenced by events and experiences. What events and experiences made you what you are today?

at home

in school

in the community